ESL Writing Activities

for

Kids and Adults

ESL Writing Activities

for

Kids and Adults

50 Fun Activities for Teaching Writing
Skills to English Language Learners

By Paul Young

Copyright © 2024 by Paul Young

All rights reserved. The activities in this book may not be reproduced, stored in a retrieval system, or transmitted, in any form or by any means, electronic, mechanical, photocopying, recording, or otherwise, without the written permission of the publisher.

ESL Writing Activities for Kids and Adults: 50 Fun Activities for Teaching Writing Skills to English Language Learners / Paul Young

ESL Expat
eslexpat.com

Contents

Introduction viii

ESL Writing Activities

1. Email Writing — 1
2. Social Media Posts — 7
3. Restaurant Review — 13
4. News Article Summary — 19
5. Diary Entry — 23
6. Movie Review — 29
7. Travel Blog — 35
8. Recipe Writing — 41
9. Cause-Effect Essay — 47
10. Product Description — 53
11. Interview Q & A — 59
12. Event Invitation — 65
13. Opinion Piece — 71
14. Advertisement — 77
15. Letter to the Editor — 83
16. Advantage-Disadvantage Essay — 89
17. How-To Guide — 95
18. Song Lyrics Analysis — 101
19. Book Review — 107
20. Character Diary — 113
21. Podcast Script — 119
22. News Report — 125
23. Travel Itinerary — 131
24. Speech Writing — 137
25. Problem-Solution Essay — 143
26. Interview Transcription — 149
27. Personal Narrative — 155
28. Annotated Bibliography — 161
29. Debate Argument — 167
30. Nature Description — 173

31. Business Proposal	179
32. Formal Complaint	185
33. Short Story	191
34. Memoir Excerpt	197
35. Photo Essay	203
36. Editorial Cartoon Analysis	209
37. Formal Report	215
38. Story Continuation	221
39. Literary Analysis	227
40. Biography	233
41. Film Scene Rewrite	239
42. FAQ Creation	245
43. Press Release	251
44. Comparative Essay	257
45. Infographic Analysis	263
46. Local Event Report	269
47. Comic Strip Dialogue	275
48. Petition Writing	281
49. Cover Letter	287
50. Resume Writing	293

ESL Books and Resources — 300

Introduction

Welcome to *ESL Writing Activities for Kids and Adults*!

This book is designed to help learners improve their writing skills through a variety of engaging and practical activities. Writing is a fundamental skill that not only aids in communication but also enhances critical thinking, creativity, and self-expression.

Whether you are a teacher looking for effective classroom activities or a learner seeking to improve your writing proficiency, this book offers a comprehensive collection of exercises tailored to diverse needs, interests, and language levels (from intermediate to advanced).

Why Focus on Writing Skills?

In today's globalized world, strong writing skills are essential for effective communication, academic success, and professional development. For English language learners (ELLs), writing serves as a critical tool for expressing ideas, sharing experiences, and engaging with diverse audiences.

Developing proficiency in writing not only enhances language abilities but also fosters critical thinking, creativity, and confidence. Writing skills are foundational to mastering other aspects of the English language, including reading comprehension and oral communication.

By focusing on writing, learners can unlock new opportunities for personal and professional growth, making it a vital component of language education.

INTRODUCTION

What to Expect from This Activity Book

A Variety of Writing Activities

This activity book is designed to provide ELLs with a comprehensive set of writing activities that use authentic content to engage and challenge learners. Each activity focuses on a different type of writing, from formal emails and cover letters to creative tasks like diary entries and short stories.

Writing Skills and Language Development

The activities are structured to build key writing skills, such as organizing ideas, developing arguments, describing experiences, and analyzing information. Learners will have the opportunity to practice writing in various contexts, enhancing their versatility and adaptability.

Guided Instruction and Peer Review

Through guided instruction, peer reviews, and reflective exercises, this book aims to support learners in becoming confident and proficient writers. Each activity includes detailed teaching outlines and assessment checklists to guide the learning process.

Engaging and Authentic Content

Learners will engage with authentic content that is relevant to their experiences and interests. This approach ensures that the writing tasks are meaningful and enjoyable, helping learners stay motivated and invested in their language development.

Introduction

How to Use This Activity Book

This activity book is designed to be flexible and user-friendly, catering to the needs of both learners and educators. Each writing activity includes a detailed teaching outline, clear instructions, and an assessment checklist to guide the learning process.

Educators can use these activities in the classroom to supplement their existing curriculum or as standalone lessons. Learners can work through the activities independently or in pairs/groups for collaborative learning. The writing tasks can be completed on a computer or on lined paper.

The book is organized to allow users to select activities based on their interests and learning goals, making it adaptable to various learning environments. In the print version of this book, use the space at the end of each writing activity for making notes.

By following the structured guidance and utilizing the provided materials, learners can systematically build their writing skills and gain confidence in their ability to communicate effectively in English.

ESL Writing Activities for Kids and Adults

Email Writing

Objective: Learners will practice writing formal emails to request information, improving their ability to communicate professionally and effectively in written English.

Level: Intermediate to Advanced

Duration: 1 hour and 30 minutes

Materials Needed

- Sample email templates
- Email Writing Checklist

Teaching Outline

Introduction (10 minutes)

Begin by discussing the importance of email in professional communication. Explain the structure of a formal email: Subject Line, Greeting, Introduction, Body, Closing, and Signature. Encourage learners to ask questions and participate actively in the discussion.

Warm-Up (10 minutes)

Display a sample formal email. Highlight the key parts of the email and discuss common phrases and language used in formal emails. Facilitate a brief role-play activity where students act out a formal email exchange.

ESL Writing Activities for Kids and Adults

Research (10 minutes)

Ask learners to choose a company they are interested in, either from a provided list or by searching online. Guide learners in conducting thorough research to gather relevant information about the chosen company's offerings.

Drafting the Email (20 minutes)

Distribute the Email Writing Checklist. Instruct learners to write their email following the formal email structure:

- Clear subject line
- Polite greeting
- Brief self-introduction
- Clear request for information
- Specific questions

Polite closing and signature. Offer support and guidance as needed to ensure that learners understand and apply the key components of formal email writing effectively.

Peer Review (15 minutes)

Have learners exchange emails with a partner. Partners review each other's emails using the Email Writing Checklist. Encourage learners to focus on both strengths and areas for improvement in their partner's email.

Final Draft (15 minutes)

Learners revise their emails based on the feedback received. They then write the final draft of the email. Encourage learners to reflect on the feedback received during the peer review process and make thoughtful revisions to their emails.

Reflection (10 minutes)

Conduct a class discussion on what they learned about writing formal emails. Facilitate a reflective discussion where learners can articulate their insights and discoveries about the email writing process.

Email Writing Checklist

Subject Line

- Is it clear and specific?
- Does it summarize the purpose of the email?

Greeting

- Is it polite and appropriate for the recipient?

Introduction

- Does it clearly state who the writer is?
- Is it concise and to the point?

Body

- Does it clearly state the request for information?
- Are specific questions about the product/service included?
- Is the language formal and polite?

Closing

- Is there a polite closing line?
- Is the writer's name included at the end of the email?

Assessment

Evaluate the learners' emails based on the clarity and specificity of the subject line, appropriateness of the greeting, quality of the introduction, effectiveness of the body in clearly requesting information and including specific, relevant questions, the politeness and formality of the language used, and the completeness of the closing, including a polite sign-off and the writer's name.

This activity helps learners develop professional communication skills by practicing formal email writing, which is crucial in professional and academic settings. It encourages critical thinking through crafting specific questions and requests.

ESL Writing Activities for Kids and Adults

Social Media Posts

Objective: Learners will practice writing concise, engaging social media posts, improving their ability to communicate effectively and appropriately in various social media contexts.

Level: Intermediate to Advanced

Duration: 1 hour and 30 minutes

Materials Needed

- Examples of social media posts (screenshots or links)
- Social Media Post Writing Checklist

Teaching Outline

Introduction (10 minutes)

Begin by discussing the role of social media in personal and professional communication. Explain the key elements of an effective social media post, including brevity, engagement, and relevance. Encourage learners to share their experiences with social media.

Warm-Up (10 minutes)

Display examples of successful social media posts from various platforms (e.g., Twitter, Facebook, Instagram). Highlight the different tones and styles used for each platform and discuss what makes these posts effective. Ask learners to identify the elements they think contribute to a post's success.

Research (10 minutes)

Ask learners to select a topic or product they are passionate about or interested in. They should research recent trends, popular hashtags, and related content on their chosen topic. Encourage them to take notes on the language and style used in popular posts.

Drafting the Post (20 minutes)

Distribute the Social Media Post Writing Checklist. Instruct learners to draft a social media post for their chosen topic. Remind them to consider:

- Platform-specific constraints (e.g., character limits for Twitter)
- Use of hashtags and mentions
- Engaging visuals or links
- A clear call to action or engaging question

Peer Review (15 minutes)

Have learners exchange posts with a partner. Partners review each other's posts using the Social Media Post Writing Checklist. Encourage learners to focus on clarity, engagement, and appropriateness for the chosen platform.

Final Draft (15 minutes)

Learners revise their posts based on the feedback received. They then write the final draft of their social media post. Optionally, they can share their posts on a class blog or social media account set up by the teacher.

Reflection (10 minutes)

Conduct a class discussion on what they learned about writing social media posts. Facilitate a reflective discussion where learners can articulate their insights and discoveries about the social media writing process.

ESL Writing Activities for Kids and Adults

Social Media Posts Writing Checklist

Clarity

- Is the message clear and easy to understand?
- Is it concise and to the point?

Engagement

- Does it include a call to action or a question to engage the audience?
- Are relevant hashtags and mentions used appropriately?

Appropriateness

- Is the tone suitable for the chosen platform?
- Is the language appropriate for the target audience?

Visuals

- If included, do the visuals enhance the message?
- Are the visuals relevant and engaging?

Assessment

Evaluate the learners' social media posts based on clarity, engagement, appropriateness for the platform, and effective use of visuals and hashtags. Consider how well they incorporated feedback from the peer review and whether their posts would likely be effective in a real social media context.

This activity helps learners develop skills in writing for social media, which is essential for both personal and professional communication in today's digital age. It encourages creative thinking through crafting engaging content across different social media platforms.

ESL Writing Activities for Kids and Adults

Restaurant Review

Objective: Learners will practice writing detailed and descriptive restaurant reviews, improving their ability to express opinions and provide useful information in written English.

Level: Intermediate to Advanced

Duration: 1 hour and 30 minutes

Materials Needed

- Sample restaurant reviews (screenshots or links)
- Restaurant Review Writing Checklist

Teaching Outline

Introduction (10 minutes)

Begin by discussing the purpose and importance of restaurant reviews. Explain the key components of a well-written restaurant review, including the description of the food, ambiance, service, and overall experience. Encourage learners to share their experiences with reading or writing reviews.

Warm-Up (10 minutes)

Display examples of detailed and well-written restaurant reviews. Highlight the different elements that make these reviews effective, such as vivid descriptions, balanced opinions, and specific details. Discuss the tone and language typically used in professional and casual reviews.

Research (10 minutes)

Ask learners to choose a restaurant they have visited recently or one they are interested in. They should gather relevant information about the restaurant, such as its menu, location, ambiance, and any unique features. Encourage them to take notes on their personal experience or the information they find online.

Drafting the Review (20 minutes)

Distribute the Restaurant Review Writing Checklist. Instruct learners to write their restaurant review, ensuring they include:

- A brief introduction to the restaurant
- Detailed descriptions of the food and drinks
- Comments on the ambiance and setting
- Observations about the service
- Their overall impression and recommendation

Peer Review (15 minutes)

Have learners exchange reviews with a partner. Partners review each other's work using the Restaurant Review Writing Checklist. Encourage learners to focus on the clarity, detail, and balance of the review, as well as the effectiveness of the descriptions.

Final Draft (15 minutes)

Learners revise their reviews based on the feedback received. They then write the final draft of their restaurant review. Optionally, they can share their reviews on a class blog or review platform set up by the teacher.

Reflection (10 minutes)

Conduct a class discussion on what they learned about writing restaurant reviews. Facilitate a reflective discussion where learners can articulate their insights and discoveries about the review writing process.

Restaurant Review Writing Checklist

Introduction

- Is there a clear introduction to the restaurant?
- Does it provide context for the review?

Food and Drinks

- Are the food and drinks described in detail?
- Are specific dishes and their flavors highlighted?

Ambiance and Setting

- Is the ambiance of the restaurant described?
- Are specific elements of the setting mentioned?

Service

- Are the observations about the service clear and detailed?
- Are both positive and negative aspects of the service mentioned?

Overall Impression

- Is there a clear overall impression of the dining experience?
- Is there a recommendation or conclusion?

Assessment

Evaluate the learners' restaurant reviews based on the clarity and detail of the introduction, descriptions of the food and drinks, comments on the ambiance and service, and the overall impression and recommendation. Consider how well they incorporated feedback from the peer review and whether their reviews provide a balanced and informative perspective on the restaurant.

This activity helps learners develop descriptive writing skills and the ability to express opinions clearly and effectively. It enhances their ability to provide detailed reviews, and encourages critical thinking through evaluating various aspects of the dining experience.

News Article Summary

Objective: Learners will practice summarizing news articles, improving their ability to identify key points and convey information concisely in written English.

Level: Intermediate to Advanced

Duration: 1 hour and 30 minutes

Materials Needed

- Sample news articles (printed or digital)
- News Article Summary Checklist

Teaching Outline

Introduction (10 minutes)

Begin by discussing the importance of summarizing news articles, such as staying informed and sharing information. Explain the key elements of a good summary: identifying main ideas, avoiding unnecessary details, and using clear and concise language. Encourage learners to share their experiences with reading and summarizing news.

Warm-Up (10 minutes)

Display a sample news article and its summary. Highlight the main points that were included in the summary and discuss why certain details were omitted. Emphasize the importance of capturing the essence of the article without adding personal opinions or interpretations.

Research (10 minutes)

Ask learners to select a recent news article from a reputable news source. They should read the article carefully, taking notes on the key points, main ideas, and important details. Encourage them to identify the who, what, when, where, why, and how of the article.

Drafting the Summary (20 minutes)

Distribute the News Article Summary Checklist. Instruct learners to write their summary, ensuring they include:

- The main idea of the article
- Key points and important details
- Clear and concise language without personal opinions

Peer Review (15 minutes)

Have learners exchange summaries with a partner. Partners review each other's work using the News Article Summary Checklist. Encourage learners to focus on the clarity and conciseness of the summary, as well as the inclusion of all key points.

Final Draft (15 minutes)

Learners revise their summaries based on the feedback received. They then write the final draft of their news article summary. Optionally, they can share their summaries in a class discussion or on a class blog.

Reflection (10 minutes)

Conduct a class discussion on what they learned about summarizing news articles. Facilitate a reflective discussion where learners can articulate their insights and discoveries about the summarizing process.

News Article Summary Checklist

Main Idea

- Is the main idea of the article clearly stated?
- Does the summary capture the essence of the article?

Key Points

- Are the key points and important details included?
- Are unnecessary details omitted?

Clarity and Conciseness

- Is the language clear and concise?
- Is the summary free of personal opinions and interpretations?

Assessment

Evaluate the learners' summaries based on the clarity and accuracy of the main idea, the inclusion of key points and important details, and the conciseness and objectivity of the language. Consider how well they incorporated feedback from the peer review and whether their summaries effectively convey the essence of the original news article.

This activity helps learners develop summarizing skills, which are essential for academic and professional communication. It enhances their ability to identify key points and convey information concisely, and encourages critical thinking through analyzing and condensing complex information.

Diary Entry

Objective: Learners will practice writing personal diary entries, improving their ability to express thoughts, feelings, and experiences in written English.

Level: Intermediate to Advanced

Duration: 1 hour and 30 minutes

Materials Needed

- Writing journals or notebooks
- Sample diary entries (printed or digital)
- Diary Entry Writing Checklist

Teaching Outline

Introduction (10 minutes)

Begin by discussing the purpose of keeping a diary, such as self-reflection, personal growth, and documenting experiences. Explain the key components of a diary entry: date, description of events, personal thoughts, and feelings. Encourage learners to share if they have ever kept a diary or journal.

Warm-Up (10 minutes)

Display a sample diary entry. Highlight the use of descriptive language, personal reflection, and emotional expression. Discuss how diary entries differ from other types of writing due to their personal and informal nature.

ESL Writing Activities for Kids and Adults

Brainstorming (10 minutes)

Ask learners to think about a recent event or day that was significant to them. They should consider what happened, how they felt, and any reflections or thoughts they had about the experience. Encourage them to jot down notes or create a mind map to organize their ideas.

Drafting the Diary Entry (20 minutes)

Distribute the Diary Entry Writing Checklist. Instruct learners to write their diary entry, ensuring they include:

- The date of the entry
- A detailed description of the event or day
- Personal thoughts and feelings about the experience
- Reflections or insights gained from the event

Peer Review (15 minutes)

Have learners exchange diary entries with a partner. Partners review each other's entries using the Diary Entry Writing Checklist. Encourage learners to focus on the clarity, detail, and emotional expression of the entry, as well as the inclusion of personal reflections.

Final Draft (15 minutes)

Learners revise their diary entries based on the feedback received. They then write the final draft of their entry. Optionally, they can share their entries in a small group or class discussion, respecting each other's privacy and confidentiality.

Reflection (10 minutes)

Conduct a class discussion on what they learned about writing diary entries. Facilitate a reflective discussion where learners can articulate their insights and discoveries about expressing personal thoughts and feelings through writing.

Diary Entry Writing Checklist

Date

- Is the date of the entry included?

Description of Events

- Is there a detailed description of the event or day?
- Are specific details and experiences mentioned?

Personal Thoughts and Feelings

- Are personal thoughts and feelings clearly expressed?
- Is the language reflective and personal?

Reflections and Insights

- Are reflections or insights about the experience included?
- Does the entry convey any lessons learned or personal growth?

Assessment

Evaluate the learners' diary entries based on the inclusion of the date, detailed description of events, clarity and depth of personal thoughts and feelings, and the inclusion of reflections or insights. Consider how well they incorporated feedback from the peer review and whether their entries effectively convey their personal experiences and reflections.

This activity helps learners develop expressive writing skills, which are essential for personal and emotional growth. It enhances their ability to reflect on and articulate their experiences and feelings, and encourages self-awareness and introspection through personal reflection.

ESL Writing Activities for Kids and Adults

Movie Review

Objective: Learners will practice writing detailed and engaging movie reviews, improving their ability to analyze and critique visual media in written English.

Level: Intermediate to Advanced

Duration: 1 hour and 30 minutes

Materials Needed

- Sample movie reviews (printed or digital)
- Movie Review Writing Checklist

Teaching Outline

Introduction (10 minutes)

Begin by discussing the purpose and importance of movie reviews, such as informing potential viewers and providing critical analysis. Explain the key components of a well-written movie review: summary, analysis, and evaluation. Encourage learners to share their experiences with reading or writing reviews.

Warm-Up (10 minutes)

Display examples of detailed and well-written movie reviews. Highlight the different elements that make these reviews effective, such as a concise summary, insightful analysis, and balanced evaluation. Discuss the tone and language typically used in professional and casual reviews.

Research (10 minutes)

Ask learners to choose a movie they have recently watched or one they are familiar with. They should gather relevant information about the movie, such as its plot, characters, director, and any notable aspects of its production. Encourage them to take notes on their personal experience and any additional information they find online.

Drafting the Review (20 minutes)

Distribute the Movie Review Writing Checklist. Instruct learners to write their movie review, ensuring they include:

- A brief summary of the movie's plot without spoilers
- Analysis of key elements such as acting, direction, cinematography, and music
- Personal evaluation and recommendation

Peer Review (15 minutes)

Have learners exchange reviews with a partner. Partners review each other's work using the Movie Review Writing Checklist. Encourage learners to focus on the clarity, detail, and balance of the review, as well as the effectiveness of the analysis and evaluation.

Final Draft (15 minutes)

Learners revise their reviews based on the feedback received. They then write the final draft of their movie review. Optionally, they can share their reviews on a class blog or movie review platform set up by the teacher.

Reflection (10 minutes)

Conduct a class discussion on what they learned about writing movie reviews. Facilitate a reflective discussion where learners can articulate their insights and discoveries about the review writing process.

Movie Review Writing Checklist

Summary

- Is there a clear and concise summary of the movie's plot?
- Does the summary avoid spoilers?

Analysis

- Are key elements of the movie (acting, direction, cinematography, music) analyzed?
- Is the analysis insightful and well-supported?

Evaluation

- Is there a personal evaluation of the movie?
- Is there a clear recommendation or conclusion?

Clarity and Balance

- Is the review clear and easy to understand?
- Does the review provide a balanced perspective?

Assessment

Evaluate the learners' movie reviews based on the clarity and conciseness of the summary, the insightfulness and support of the analysis, the balance and clarity of the evaluation, and the overall effectiveness of the review. Consider how well they incorporated feedback from the peer review and whether their reviews provide a balanced and informative perspective on the movie.

This activity helps learners develop critical thinking and analytical writing skills, which are essential for academic and professional communication. It enhances their ability to articulate and support their opinions, and encourages attention to detail through analyzing various aspects of a movie.

Travel Blog

Objective: Learners will practice writing engaging and informative travel blog posts, improving their ability to describe experiences and convey useful information in written English.

Level: Intermediate to Advanced

Duration: 1 hour and 30 minutes

Materials Needed

- Sample travel blog posts (printed or digital)
- Travel Blog Writing Checklist

Teaching Outline

Introduction (10 minutes)

Begin by discussing the purpose and appeal of travel blogs, such as sharing experiences, providing travel tips, and inspiring others. Explain the key components of a well-written travel blog post: engaging introduction, vivid descriptions, practical information, and personal reflections. Encourage learners to share their experiences with reading or writing travel blogs.

Warm-Up (10 minutes)

Display examples of detailed and engaging travel blog posts. Highlight the different elements that make these posts effective, such as descriptive language, personal anecdotes, and useful travel tips. Discuss the tone and style typically used in travel writing, which often blends informative and narrative elements.

Research (10 minutes)

Ask learners to choose a travel destination they have visited or wish to visit. They should gather relevant information about the destination, such as its attractions, culture, history, and practical travel tips. Encourage them to take notes on their personal experiences or the information they find online.

Drafting the Blog Post (20 minutes)

Distribute the Travel Blog Writing Checklist. Instruct learners to write their travel blog post, ensuring they include:

- An engaging introduction that captures the reader's interest
- Vivid descriptions of the destination and experiences
- Practical travel tips and useful information
- Personal reflections and anecdotes

Peer Review (15 minutes)

Have learners exchange blog posts with a partner. Partners review each other's work using the Travel Blog Writing Checklist. Encourage learners to focus on the clarity, detail, and engagement of the post, as well as the inclusion of practical tips and personal reflections.

Final Draft (15 minutes)

Learners revise their blog posts based on the feedback received. They then write the final draft of their travel blog post. Optionally, they can share their posts on a class blog or travel blog platform set up by the teacher.

Reflection (10 minutes)

Conduct a class discussion on what they learned about writing travel blogs. Facilitate a reflective discussion where learners can articulate their insights and discoveries about the travel blogging process.

ESL Writing Activities for Kids and Adults

Travel Blog Writing Checklist

Introduction

- Is the introduction engaging and does it capture the reader's interest?
- Does it provide a clear context for the blog post?

Descriptions

- Are the descriptions of the destination vivid and detailed?
- Do the descriptions effectively convey the atmosphere and experiences?

Practical Tips

- Are practical travel tips and useful information included?
- Are the tips relevant and helpful for potential travelers?

Personal Reflections

- Are personal reflections and anecdotes included?
- Do the reflections add a personal touch to the blog post?

Clarity and Engagement

- Is the blog post clear and easy to understand?
- Is the writing engaging and does it hold the reader's interest?

Assessment

Evaluate the learners' travel blog posts based on the engagement and clarity of the introduction, the vividness and detail of the descriptions, the relevance and usefulness of the practical tips, and the depth of personal reflections and anecdotes. Consider how well they incorporated feedback from the peer review and whether their posts effectively convey their travel experiences and information in an engaging manner.

This activity helps learners develop descriptive and narrative writing skills, which are essential for personal and professional communication. It enhances their ability to share experiences and convey useful information, and encourages creativity and attention to detail through descriptive writing.

Recipe Writing

Objective: Learners will practice writing clear and detailed recipes, improving their ability to convey instructions and information in written English.

Level: Intermediate to Advanced

Duration: 1 hour and 30 minutes

Materials Needed

- Sample recipes (printed or digital)
- Recipe Writing Checklist

Teaching Outline

Introduction (10 minutes)

Begin by discussing the purpose and importance of writing clear and accurate recipes, such as sharing culinary knowledge and ensuring successful cooking outcomes. Explain the key components of a well-written recipe: title, ingredients list, step-by-step instructions, and additional tips. Encourage learners to share their experiences with following or writing recipes.

Warm-Up (10 minutes)

Display examples of clear and well-structured recipes. Highlight the different elements that make these recipes effective, such as precise measurements, step-by-step instructions, and helpful tips. Discuss the importance of clarity and detail in recipe writing to ensure the reader can successfully recreate the dish.

Choosing a Recipe (10 minutes)

Ask learners to think of a dish they enjoy making or would like to share. They should consider the ingredients, steps involved, and any tips or variations they want to include. Encourage them to jot down notes or create a rough outline of their recipe.

Drafting the Recipe (20 minutes)

Distribute the Recipe Writing Checklist. Instruct learners to write their recipe, ensuring they include:

- A clear and descriptive title
- A detailed list of ingredients with precise measurements
- Step-by-step instructions for preparing the dish
- Additional tips or variations, if applicable

Peer Review (15 minutes)

Have learners exchange recipes with a partner. Partners review each other's work using the Recipe Writing Checklist. Encourage learners to focus on the clarity and completeness of the ingredients list, the detail and sequence of the instructions, and the usefulness of any additional tips.

Final Draft (15 minutes)

Learners revise their recipes based on the feedback received. They then write the final draft of their recipe. Optionally, they can share their recipes in a class cookbook or online recipe platform set up by the teacher.

Reflection (10 minutes)

Conduct a class discussion on what they learned about writing recipes. Facilitate a reflective discussion where learners can articulate their insights and discoveries about the recipe writing process.

Recipe Writing Checklist

Title

- Is the title clear and descriptive?
- Does it accurately reflect the dish?

Ingredients List

- Are all ingredients listed with precise measurements?
- Are any special preparation instructions for the ingredients included?

Instructions

- Are the instructions clear and easy to follow?
- Are the steps listed in the correct order?
- Are specific cooking times, temperatures, and techniques included?

Additional Tips

- Are any additional tips or variations provided?
- Are these tips helpful and relevant to the recipe?

Assessment

Evaluate the learners' recipes based on the clarity and descriptiveness of the title, the precision and completeness of the ingredients list, the clarity and sequence of the instructions, and the usefulness of any additional tips. Consider how well they incorporated feedback from the peer review and whether their recipes provide clear and detailed guidance for recreating the dish.

This activity helps learners develop technical writing skills, which are essential for clear and effective communication. It enhances their ability to convey detailed instructions and information, and encourages attention to detail through precise measurement and sequencing.

ESL Writing Activities for Kids and Adults

Cause-Effect Essay

Objective: Learners will practice writing a cause-effect essay to enhance their ability to analyze relationships between events and present their analysis clearly and effectively in written English.

Level: Intermediate to Advanced

Duration: 2 hours

Materials Needed

- Examples of cause-effect essays (printed or digital)
- Cause-Effect Essay Writing Checklist

Teaching Outline

Introduction (10 minutes)

Start by explaining the purpose and structure of a cause-effect essay. Highlight that these essays analyze the reasons why something happens (causes) and the results of those happenings (effects). Discuss the importance of a clear thesis statement that outlines the focus of the essay, logical organization, and the use of evidence to support the analysis.

Warm-Up (10 minutes)

Present examples of well-written cause-effect essays. Discuss their key elements, such as a strong introduction with a thesis statement, body paragraphs that clearly explain causes and effects, and a conclusion that summarizes the analysis. Highlight the importance of using clear and concise language to explain the relationships between events.

Choosing a Topic (10 minutes)

Ask learners to choose a topic they are interested in that has clear cause-and-effect relationships. These could be related to social issues, historical events, natural phenomena, personal experiences, etc. Ensure that learners choose topics with enough depth to analyze in detail.

Planning the Essay (15 minutes)

Distribute the Cause-Effect Essay Writing Checklist. Instruct learners to outline their essay, including the following sections:

- **Introduction:** Introduce the topic and present a clear thesis statement.
- **Body Paragraphs:** Organize the body paragraphs to explain the causes of the event and the effects of those causes. This can be done in separate paragraphs or within the same paragraphs, depending on the complexity of the topic.
- **Conclusion:** Summarize the main points of the essay and restate the thesis in a new light.

Writing the Draft (25 minutes)

Learners write the first draft of their cause-effect essay based on their outline. Encourage them to focus on providing clear explanations of the causes and effects, using evidence and examples to support their analysis. Remind them to maintain coherence and logical flow throughout the essay.

Peer Review (20 minutes)

Have learners exchange their essays with a partner. Partners review each other's work using the Cause-Effect Essay Writing Checklist. Encourage learners to provide constructive feedback on the clarity and coherence of the essay, the strength of the analysis, and the organization of the content.

Final Draft (20 minutes)

Learners revise their essays based on the feedback received. They then write the final draft of their cause-effect essay, ensuring that it is well-organized, clearly written, and effectively analyzes the relationships between events. Optionally, they can share their essays with the class, practicing their presentation and communication skills.

Reflection (10 minutes)

Conduct a class discussion on what they learned about writing cause-effect essays. Facilitate a reflective discussion where learners can articulate their insights and discoveries about analyzing relationships between events, using evidence to support their analysis, and organizing essays effectively.

Cause-Effect Essay Writing Checklist

Introduction

- Does the introduction provide a clear overview of the topic?
- Is there a strong thesis statement that outlines the main points of the essay?

Body Paragraphs

- Are the causes and effects clearly explained and well-supported with evidence and examples?
- Is there a logical progression from one point to the next?
- Are transitions between paragraphs smooth and coherent?

Conclusion

- Does the conclusion summarize the main points of the essay?
- Is the thesis restated in a new light?
- Are the final thoughts insightful and conclusive?

Clarity and Accuracy

- Is the essay written in a clear and concise manner?
- Is the information accurate and free of errors?

Organization and Flow

- Is the essay well-organized and logically structured?
- Are transitions between sections smooth and coherent?

Assessment

Evaluate the learners' essays based on the clarity and accuracy of the introduction, the effectiveness and coherence of the body paragraphs, the relevance and clarity of the conclusion, and the overall organization and flow of the essay. Consider how well they incorporated feedback from the peer review and whether their essays effectively analyze the cause-effect relationships.

This activity helps learners develop analytical and critical thinking skills by exploring the relationships between causes and effects. By practicing cause-effect essay writing, learners improve their ability to analyze situations and articulate their thoughts in a structured and coherent manner.

ESL Writing Activities for Kids and Adults

Product Description

Objective: Learners will practice writing clear and engaging product descriptions, improving their ability to convey detailed information and persuasive content in written English.

Level: Intermediate to Advanced

Duration: 1 hour and 30 minutes

Materials Needed

- Sample product descriptions (printed or digital)
- Product Description Writing Checklist

Teaching Outline

Introduction (10 minutes)

Begin by discussing the purpose and importance of product descriptions, such as informing potential buyers and encouraging purchases. Explain the key components of an effective product description: product features, benefits, specifications, and persuasive language. Encourage learners to share their experiences with reading or writing product descriptions.

Warm-Up (10 minutes)

Display examples of clear and compelling product descriptions. Highlight the different elements that make these descriptions effective, such as detailed features, clear benefits, and engaging language. Discuss the importance of using descriptive and persuasive language to appeal to potential buyers.

Choosing a Product (10 minutes)

Ask learners to think of a product they own or are familiar with, or they can select a product from an online store. They should consider the product's features, benefits, and any unique selling points. Encourage them to take notes on these aspects to help structure their description.

Drafting the Product Description (20 minutes)

Distribute the Product Description Writing Checklist. Instruct learners to write their product description, ensuring they include:

- A clear and descriptive product title
- Detailed features of the product
- The benefits of these features to the user
- Any necessary specifications or technical details
- Persuasive language to engage potential buyers

Peer Review (15 minutes)

Have learners exchange product descriptions with a partner. Partners review each other's work using the Product Description Writing Checklist. Encourage learners to focus on the clarity and detail of the features and benefits, the accuracy of specifications, and the effectiveness of the persuasive language.

Final Draft (15 minutes)

Learners revise their product descriptions based on the feedback received. They then write the final draft of their description. Optionally, they can share their descriptions in a small group or class discussion, simulating a product pitch.

Reflection (10 minutes)

Conduct a class discussion on what they learned about writing product descriptions. Facilitate a reflective discussion where learners can articulate their insights and discoveries about the product description writing process.

Product Description Writing Checklist

Title

- Is the product title clear and descriptive?
- Does it capture the essence of the product?

Features

- Are the key features of the product clearly listed?
- Are the features detailed and specific?

Benefits

- Are the benefits of each feature clearly explained?
- Do the benefits address potential customer needs or desires?

Specifications

- Are any necessary specifications or technical details included?
- Are the specifications accurate and relevant?

Persuasive Language

- Is the language engaging and persuasive?
- Does the description encourage potential buyers to purchase the product?

Clarity and Accuracy

- Is the description free of spelling and grammatical errors?
- Is the information accurate and well-organized?

Assessment

Evaluate the learners' product descriptions based on the clarity and descriptiveness of the title, the detail and specificity of the features, the effectiveness of the benefits in addressing customer needs, the accuracy and relevance of the specifications, and the engagement and persuasiveness of the language. Consider how well they incorporated feedback from the peer review and whether their descriptions effectively present the product to potential buyers.

This activity helps learners develop descriptive and persuasive writing skills, which are essential for marketing and sales communication. It enhances their ability to convey detailed product information and persuade potential buyers.

Interview Q & A

Objective: Learners will practice writing thoughtful and effective interview questions and answers, improving their ability to conduct and participate in interviews in written English.

Level: Intermediate to Advanced

Duration: 1 hour and 30 minutes

Materials Needed

- Sample interview questions and answers (printed or digital)
- Interview Q & A Writing Checklist

Teaching Outline

Introduction (10 minutes)

Begin by discussing the importance of well-prepared interview questions and answers, such as gaining insights and making a good impression. Explain the key components of effective interview questions: open-ended, clear, and relevant to the topic. For responses, emphasize the need for clarity, detail, and relevance. Encourage learners to share their experiences with conducting or participating in interviews.

Warm-Up (10 minutes)

Display examples of effective interview questions and detailed responses. Highlight the different elements that make these questions and responses effective, such as being open-ended for questions and being specific and detailed for responses. Discuss the importance of preparation and thoughtfulness in both asking and answering questions.

Choosing an Interview Topic (10 minutes)

Ask learners to choose a topic for their interview, such as a job interview, an informational interview, or a journalistic interview. They should consider the purpose of the interview and the type of information they want to obtain or convey. Encourage them to take notes on the key points and focus areas.

Drafting Interview Questions (10 minutes)

Distribute the Interview Q & A Writing Checklist. Instruct learners to write their interview questions, ensuring they include:

- A clear and relevant introduction explaining the purpose of the interview
- Open-ended questions that encourage detailed responses
- Follow-up questions to delve deeper into specific areas

Drafting Interview Responses (10 minutes)

Next, learners will write responses to the questions they have created, ensuring they include:

- Clear and detailed answers that provide useful information
- Relevant examples or anecdotes to illustrate their points
- A closing statement that summarizes their key points and reinforces their message

Peer Review (15 minutes)

Have learners exchange interview questions and responses with a partner. Partners review each other's work using the Interview Q & A

Writing Checklist. Encourage learners to focus on the clarity and relevance of the questions, the detail and specificity of the responses, and the overall coherence and flow of the interview.

Final Draft (15 minutes)

Learners revise their questions and responses based on the feedback received. They then write the final draft of their interview questions and responses. Optionally, they can conduct a mock interview in pairs or small groups to practice asking and answering their questions.

Reflection (10 minutes)

Conduct a class discussion on what they learned about writing interview questions and answers. Facilitate a reflective discussion where learners can articulate their insights and discoveries about the interview preparation and execution process.

Interview Q & A Writing Checklist

Questions

- Are the questions clear and relevant to the interview topic?
- Are the questions open-ended and encourage detailed responses?
- Do the questions include follow-up prompts to delve deeper into specific areas?

Answers

- Are the answers clear and detailed?
- Do the answers include relevant examples or anecdotes?
- Does the closing statement summarize key points and reinforce the message?

Clarity and Relevance

- Are the questions and responses free of spelling and grammatical errors?
- Is the information well-organized and coherent?

Assessment

Evaluate the learners' interview questions and answers based on the clarity and relevance of the questions, the detail and specificity of the responses, the inclusion of relevant examples or anecdotes, and the overall coherence and flow of the interview. Consider how well they incorporated feedback from the peer review and whether their questions and responses effectively achieve the purpose of the interview.

This activity helps learners develop critical thinking and communication skills, which are essential for effective interviews. It enhances their ability to ask thoughtful questions and provide detailed, relevant responses. Additionally, it gives them experience participating in interviews for real-world applications.

ESL Writing Activities for Kids and Adults

ESL Writing Activities for Kids and Adults

Event Invitation

Objective: Learners will practice writing clear and engaging event invitations, improving their ability to convey essential information and encourage attendance in written English.

Level: Intermediate to Advanced

Duration: 1 hour and 30 minutes

Materials Needed

- Sample event invitations (printed or digital)
- Event Invitation Writing Checklist

Teaching Outline

Introduction (10 minutes)

Begin by discussing the importance of a well-written event invitation, such as providing essential information and encouraging attendance. Explain the key components of an effective event invitation: a clear purpose, event details (date, time, location), RSVP information, and an engaging tone. Encourage learners to share their experiences with receiving or writing event invitations.

Warm-Up (10 minutes)

Display examples of clear and engaging event invitations. Highlight the different elements that make these invitations effective, such as a compelling opening, detailed event information, and a call to action.

Discuss the importance of making the invitation both informative and appealing.

Choosing an Event (10 minutes)

Ask learners to think of an event they would like to invite others to, such as a party, meeting, or workshop. They should consider the purpose of the event, the target audience, and the key details that need to be included in the invitation. Encourage them to take notes on these aspects to help structure their invitation.

Drafting the Event Invitation (20 minutes)

Distribute the Event Invitation Writing Checklist. Instruct learners to write their event invitation, ensuring they include:

- A compelling opening that captures the reader's interest
- Clear and detailed event information (date, time, location)
- The purpose of the event and any special activities or highlights
- RSVP information, including how and by when to respond
- A polite and engaging closing that encourages attendance

Peer Review (15 minutes)

Have learners exchange invitations with a partner. Partners review each other's work using the Event Invitation Writing Checklist. Encourage learners to focus on the clarity and completeness of the event details, the effectiveness of the opening and closing, and the overall appeal of the invitation.

Final Draft (15 minutes)

Learners revise their invitations based on the feedback received. They then write the final draft of their event invitation. Optionally, they can share their invitations in a small group or class discussion, simulating sending and receiving invitations.

Reflection (10 minutes)

Conduct a class discussion on what they learned about writing event invitations. Facilitate a reflective discussion where learners can articulate their insights and discoveries about the event invitation writing process.

Event Invitation Writing Checklist

Opening

- Is the opening compelling and does it capture the reader's interest?
- Does it clearly introduce the event?

Event Details

- Are the date, time, and location of the event clearly stated?
- Is the purpose of the event and any special activities or highlights explained?

RSVP Information

- Is clear information provided on how and by when to respond?
- Are any additional instructions for the RSVP process included?

Closing

- Is the closing polite and does it encourage attendance?
- Does it provide a positive and engaging end to the invitation?

Clarity and Appeal

- Is the invitation free of spelling and grammatical errors?
- Is the information well-organized and easy to understand?
- Is the tone engaging and appropriate for the event?

Assessment

Evaluate the learners' event invitations based on the clarity and appeal of the opening, the completeness and detail of the event information, the clarity and instructions of the RSVP information, and the politeness and encouragement of the closing. Consider how well they incorporated feedback from the peer review and whether their invitations effectively convey the necessary information and encourage attendance.

This activity helps learners develop informative and persuasive writing skills, which are essential for effective communication. It enhances their ability to convey essential event details clearly and encourages attention to detail through accurate and well-organized writing.

Opinion Piece

Objective: Learners will practice writing well-structured opinion pieces, improving their ability to present arguments and persuade readers in written English.

Level: Intermediate to Advanced

Duration: 1 hour and 30 minutes

Materials Needed

- Sample opinion pieces (printed or digital)
- Opinion Piece Writing Checklist

Teaching Outline

Introduction (10 minutes)

Begin by discussing the purpose and importance of opinion pieces, such as influencing public opinion, sparking debate, and expressing personal views. Explain the key components of an effective opinion piece: a clear thesis statement, supporting arguments, evidence, and a compelling conclusion. Encourage learners to share their experiences with reading or writing opinion pieces.

Warm-Up (10 minutes)

Display examples of clear and persuasive opinion pieces. Highlight the different elements that make these pieces effective, such as a strong thesis, well-supported arguments, and a logical structure. Discuss the importance of expressing opinions clearly and supporting them with facts and examples.

Choosing a Topic (10 minutes)

Ask learners to think of a topic they are passionate about or have strong opinions on. They should consider current events, social issues, or personal interests. Encourage them to take notes on their main argument and the key points they want to make.

Drafting the Opinion Piece (20 minutes)

Distribute the Opinion Piece Writing Checklist. Instruct learners to write their opinion piece, ensuring they include:

- A clear thesis statement that expresses their main argument
- Several paragraphs that present their supporting arguments and evidence
- Relevant facts, examples, and quotes to support their arguments
- A compelling conclusion that summarizes their points and reinforces their thesis

Peer Review (15 minutes)

Have learners exchange opinion pieces with a partner. Partners review each other's work using the Opinion Piece Writing Checklist. Encourage learners to focus on the clarity and strength of the thesis, the relevance and support of the arguments, the use of evidence, and the overall persuasiveness of the piece.

Final Draft (15 minutes)

Learners revise their opinion pieces based on the feedback received. They then write the final draft of their opinion piece. Optionally, they can share their pieces in a small group or class discussion, simulating a debate or editorial review.

Reflection (10 minutes)

Conduct a class discussion on what they learned about writing opinion pieces. Facilitate a reflective discussion where learners can articulate their insights and discoveries about the opinion writing process.

Opinion Piece Writing Checklist

Thesis Statement

- Is the thesis statement clear and does it express the main argument?
- Does it set the tone and direction for the piece?

Supporting Arguments

- Are the supporting arguments clear and logically structured?
- Do they directly support the thesis statement?

Evidence

- Are relevant facts, examples, and quotes included to support the arguments?
- Is the evidence credible and well-integrated into the piece?

Conclusion

- Does the conclusion effectively summarize the main points?
- Does it reinforce the thesis and leave a lasting impression?

Clarity and Persuasiveness

- Is the opinion piece free of spelling and grammatical errors?
- Is the information well-organized and easy to follow?
- Is the tone persuasive and appropriate for the topic?

Assessment

Evaluate the learners' opinion pieces based on the clarity and strength of the thesis statement, the logical structure and relevance of the supporting arguments, the quality and integration of evidence, and the effectiveness of the conclusion. Consider how well they incorporated feedback from the peer review and whether their pieces effectively present and support their opinions.

This activity helps learners develop persuasive writing skills, which are essential for influencing and engaging readers. It enhances their ability to express opinions clearly and support them with credible evidence. Additionally, it encourages critical thinking through the development and presentation of arguments for real-world use.

Advertisement

Objective: Learners will practice writing persuasive advertisements, improving their ability to create engaging and effective marketing content in written English.

Level: Intermediate to Advanced

Duration: 1 hour and 30 minutes

Materials Needed

- Sample advertisements (printed or digital)
- Advertisement Writing Checklist

Teaching Outline

Introduction (10 minutes)

Begin by discussing the purpose and importance of advertisements, such as attracting customers and promoting products or services. Explain the key components of an effective advertisement: a catchy headline, engaging copy, key features and benefits, a call to action, and visual appeal. Encourage learners to share their experiences with advertisements they found particularly effective or memorable.

Warm-Up (10 minutes)

Display examples of clear and persuasive advertisements. Highlight the different elements that make these ads effective, such as attention-grabbing headlines, concise and engaging copy, and strong calls to action. Discuss the importance of making the advertisement appealing and informative.

Choosing a Product or Service (10 minutes)

Ask learners to choose a product or service they would like to advertise. They should consider the target audience, key features and benefits of the product or service, and the message they want to convey. Encourage them to take notes on these aspects to help structure their advertisement.

Drafting the Advertisement (20 minutes)

Distribute the Advertisement Writing Checklist. Instruct learners to write their advertisement, ensuring they include:

- A catchy headline that grabs attention
- Engaging copy that highlights the key features and benefits of the product or service
- Persuasive language that appeals to the target audience
- A strong call to action that encourages the reader to take the next step
- Any necessary contact information or details

Peer Review (15 minutes)

Have learners exchange advertisements with a partner. Partners review each other's work using the Advertisement Writing Checklist. Encourage learners to focus on the effectiveness of the headline, the clarity and engagement of the copy, the persuasiveness of the language, and the strength of the call to action.

Final Draft (15 minutes)

Learners revise their advertisements based on the feedback received. They then write the final draft of their advertisement. Optionally, they can share their advertisements in a small group or class discussion, simulating a marketing pitch.

Reflection (10 minutes)

Conduct a class discussion on what they learned about writing advertisements. Facilitate a reflective discussion where learners can articulate their insights and discoveries about the advertisement writing process.

Advertisement Writing Checklist

Headline

- Is the headline catchy and attention-grabbing?
- Does it clearly convey the main message of the advertisement?

Copy

- Is the copy engaging and does it highlight the key features and benefits of the product or service?
- Is the language persuasive and appropriate for the target audience?

Call to Action

- Is there a strong call to action that encourages the reader to take the next step?
- Are any necessary details or contact information included?

Clarity and Appeal

- Is the advertisement free of spelling and grammatical errors?
- Is the information well-organized and easy to understand?
- Is the overall tone and design appealing and suitable for the product or service?

Assessment

Evaluate the learners' advertisements based on the effectiveness of the headline, the clarity and engagement of the copy, the persuasiveness of the language, and the strength of the call to action. Consider how well they incorporated feedback from the peer review and whether their advertisements effectively attract and persuade the target audience.

This activity helps learners develop persuasive writing skills, which are essential for marketing and promotional communication. It enhances their ability to create engaging and effective advertisements, and encourages attention to detail through clear and well-organized writing.

Letter to the Editor

Objective: Learners will practice writing persuasive letters to the editor, improving their ability to express opinions, provide arguments, and engage with public discourse in written English.

Level: Intermediate to Advanced

Duration: 1 hour and 30 minutes

Materials Needed

- Sample letters to the editor (printed or digital)
- Letter to the Editor Writing Checklist

Teaching Outline

Introduction (10 minutes)

Begin by discussing the purpose and importance of letters to the editor, such as voicing opinions, influencing public opinion, and responding to articles or issues. Explain the key components of an effective letter to the editor: a clear introduction, a concise argument, supporting evidence, and a strong conclusion. Encourage learners to share their experiences with reading or writing letters to the editor.

Warm-Up (10 minutes)

Display examples of clear and persuasive letters to the editor. Highlight the different elements that make these letters effective, such as a strong opening statement, well-supported arguments, and a concise conclusion.

Discuss the importance of being clear and persuasive while maintaining a respectful tone.

Choosing a Topic (10 minutes)

Ask learners to think of a topic they feel strongly about or an article they want to respond to. They should consider current events, social issues, or local community matters. Encourage them to take notes on their main argument, supporting points, and any relevant evidence they want to include.

Drafting the Letter to the Editor (20 minutes)

Distribute the Letter to the Editor Writing Checklist. Instruct learners to write their letter, ensuring they include:

- A clear introduction that states the purpose of the letter
- A concise argument that expresses their main point
- Supporting evidence, such as facts, examples, or personal anecdotes
- A strong conclusion that summarizes their argument and suggests a call to action or final thought

Peer Review (15 minutes)

Have learners exchange letters with a partner. Partners review each other's work using the Letter to the Editor Writing Checklist. Encourage learners to focus on the clarity and strength of the argument, the relevance and support of the evidence, and the overall persuasiveness and tone of the letter.

Final Draft (15 minutes)

Learners revise their letters based on the feedback received. They then write the final draft of their letter to the editor. Optionally, they can share their letters in a small group or class discussion, simulating a public forum or editorial review.

Reflection (10 minutes)

Conduct a class discussion on what they learned about writing letters to the editor. Facilitate a reflective discussion where learners can articulate their insights and discoveries about the letter writing process and its impact on public discourse.

Letter to the Editor Writing Checklist

Introduction

- Is the introduction clear and does it state the purpose of the letter?
- Does it engage the reader and set the tone for the argument?

Argument

- Is the main argument clear and concise?
- Is it persuasive and logically structured?

Evidence

- Are relevant facts, examples, or personal anecdotes included to support the argument?
- Is the evidence credible and well-integrated into the letter?

Conclusion

- Does the conclusion effectively summarize the main points?
- Does it suggest a call to action or leave a strong final thought?

Clarity and Tone

- Is the letter free of spelling and grammatical errors?
- Is the information well-organized and easy to understand?
- Is the tone respectful and appropriate for the audience?

Assessment

Evaluate the learners' letters to the editor based on the clarity and strength of the introduction, the persuasiveness of the argument, the relevance and support of the evidence, and the effectiveness of the conclusion. Consider how well they incorporated feedback from the peer review and whether their letters effectively engage with the topic and audience.

This activity helps learners develop persuasive writing skills, which are essential for engaging in public discourse. It enhances their ability to express opinions clearly and support them with credible evidence. Furthermore, practicing in a supportive environment builds learners' confidence in their ability to write compelling letters.

ESL Writing Activities for Kids and Adults

Advantage-Disadvantage Essay

Objective: Learners will practice writing an advantage-disadvantage essay to enhance their ability to analyze both positive and negative aspects of a given topic and present their analysis clearly and effectively in written English.

Level: Intermediate to Advanced

Duration: 2 hours

Materials Needed

- Examples of advantage-disadvantage essays (printed or digital)
- Advantage-Disadvantage Essay Writing Checklist

Teaching Outline

Introduction (10 minutes)

Begin by explaining the purpose and structure of an advantage-disadvantage essay. Highlight that these essays explore both the positive and negative aspects of a topic, providing a balanced analysis. Discuss the importance of a clear thesis statement, logical organization, and the use of evidence to support the analysis.

Warm-Up (10 minutes)

Present examples of well-written advantage-disadvantage essays. Discuss their key elements, such as a strong introduction with a thesis statement, body paragraphs that explore advantages and disadvantages, and a conclusion that summarizes the analysis. Highlight the importance of using clear and concise language and providing balanced arguments.

Choosing a Topic (10 minutes)

Ask learners to choose a topic they are interested in that has clear advantages and disadvantages. These could be related to technology, social issues, policies, personal decisions, etc. Ensure that learners choose topics with enough depth to analyze in detail.

Planning the Essay (15 minutes)

Distribute the Advantage-Disadvantage Essay Writing Checklist. Instruct learners to outline their essay, including the following sections:

- **Introduction:** Introduce the topic and present a clear thesis statement that indicates the presence of both advantages and disadvantages.
- **Body Paragraphs:** Organize the body paragraphs to discuss the advantages first and then the disadvantages (or vice versa). Use evidence and examples to support the analysis.
- **Conclusion:** Summarize the main points of the essay and restate the thesis in a new light. Provide a balanced view or a final opinion based on the analysis.

Writing the Draft (25 minutes)

Learners write the first draft of their advantage-disadvantage essay based on their outline. Encourage them to focus on providing clear and balanced arguments, using evidence and examples to support their analysis. Remind them to maintain coherence and logical flow throughout the essay.

Peer Review (20 minutes)

Have learners exchange their essays with a partner. Partners review each other's work using the Advantage-Disadvantage Essay Writing Checklist. Encourage learners to provide constructive feedback on the clarity and coherence of the essay, the strength of the arguments, and the balance between the advantages and disadvantages.

Final Draft (20 minutes)

Learners revise their essays based on the feedback received. They then write the final draft of their advantage-disadvantage essay, ensuring that it is well-organized, clearly written, and effectively analyzes both the positive and negative aspects of the topic. Optionally, they can share their essays with the class, practicing their presentation and communication skills.

Reflection (10 minutes)

Conduct a class discussion on what they learned about writing advantage-disadvantage essays. Facilitate a reflective discussion where learners can articulate their insights and discoveries about analyzing topics from multiple perspectives and organizing essays effectively.

Advantage-Disadvantage Essay Writing Checklist

Introduction

- Does the introduction provide a clear overview of the topic?
- Is there a strong thesis statement that outlines the main points of the essay?

Body Paragraphs

- Are the advantages and disadvantages clearly explained and well-supported with evidence and examples?
- Is there a logical progression from one point to the next?
- Are transitions between paragraphs smooth and coherent?

Conclusion

- Does the conclusion summarize the main points of the essay?
- Is the thesis restated in a new light?
- Is there a balanced view or final opinion based on the analysis?

Clarity and Accuracy

- Is the essay written in a clear and concise manner?
- Is the information accurate and free of errors?

Organization and Flow

- Is the essay well-organized and logically structured?
- Are transitions between sections smooth and coherent?

Assessment

Evaluate the learners' essays based on the clarity and accuracy of the introduction, the effectiveness and coherence of the body paragraphs, the relevance and clarity of the conclusion, and the overall organization and flow of the essay. Consider how well they incorporated feedback from the peer review and whether their essays effectively analyze both the advantages and disadvantages of the topic.

This activity helps learners develop analytical and balanced writing skills by practicing how to explore both the positive and negative aspects of a topic. By writing advantage-disadvantage essays, learners improve their critical thinking skills and their ability to communicate complex ideas effectively.

How-To Guide

Objective: Learners will practice writing clear and detailed how-to guides, improving their ability to provide instructions and explain processes in written English.

Level: Intermediate to Advanced

Duration: 1 hour and 30 minutes

Materials Needed

- Sample how-to guides (printed or digital)
- How-To Guide Writing Checklist

Teaching Outline

Introduction (10 minutes)

Begin by discussing the purpose and importance of how-to guides, such as providing step-by-step instructions and helping readers accomplish tasks. Explain the key components of an effective how-to guide: a clear introduction, step-by-step instructions, necessary materials or tools, tips, and a conclusion. Encourage learners to share their experiences with using or writing how-to guides.

Warm-Up (10 minutes)

Display examples of clear and effective how-to guides. Highlight the different elements that make these guides useful, such as simple and direct language, logical sequence of steps, and helpful visuals or tips.

Discuss the importance of making instructions easy to follow and comprehensive.

Choosing a Topic (10 minutes)

Ask learners to think of a task or process they know well and would like to explain to others. They should consider everyday tasks, hobbies, or skills they possess. Encourage them to take notes on the necessary steps, materials, and any tips or warnings related to the task.

Drafting the How-To Guide (20 minutes)

Distribute the How-To Guide Writing Checklist. Instruct learners to write their how-to guide, ensuring they include:

- A clear introduction that explains the purpose of the guide and what the reader will achieve
- A list of necessary materials or tools
- Step-by-step instructions that are easy to follow and logically ordered
- Tips, warnings, or additional information that might help the reader
- A conclusion that summarizes the process and provides any final advice

Peer Review (15 minutes)

Have learners exchange how-to guides with a partner. Partners review each other's work using the How-To Guide Writing Checklist. Encourage learners to focus on the clarity and completeness of the instructions, the logical flow of steps, the helpfulness of tips, and the overall readability of the guide.

Final Draft (15 minutes)

Learners revise their how-to guides based on the feedback received. They then write the final draft of their guide. Optionally, they can share their guides in a small group or class discussion, simulating a workshop or instructional session.

Reflection (10 minutes)

Conduct a class discussion on what they learned about writing how-to guides. Facilitate a reflective discussion where learners can articulate their insights and discoveries about the guide writing process.

How-To Guide Writing Checklist

Introduction

- Is the introduction clear and does it explain the purpose?
- Does it inform the reader about what they will achieve?

Materials/Tools

- Is there a complete list of necessary materials or tools?
- Are the materials or tools clearly specified and described?

Instructions

- Are the step-by-step instructions clear and easy to follow?
- Are the steps logically ordered and comprehensive?

Tips/Warnings

- Are helpful tips or warnings included to assist the reader?
- Is additional information relevant and useful?

Conclusion

- Does the conclusion effectively summarize the process?
- Does it provide any final advice or encouragement?

Clarity and Readability

- Is the guide free of spelling and grammatical errors?
- Is the information well-organized and easy to understand?
- Are any visuals or diagrams clear and helpful (if included)?

Assessment

Evaluate the learners' how-to guides based on the clarity and completeness of the introduction, the detail and relevance of the materials/tools list, the logical flow and clarity of the step-by-step instructions, the helpfulness of tips and warnings, and the effectiveness of the conclusion. Consider how well they incorporated feedback from the peer review and whether their guides effectively help the reader accomplish the task.

This activity helps learners develop instructional writing skills, which are essential for effectively communicating processes and tasks. It enhances their ability to provide clear and detailed instructions, and encourages attention to detail through logical comprehensive writing.

Song Lyrics Analysis

Objective: Learners will practice analyzing song lyrics, improving their ability to interpret meaning, identify poetic devices, and appreciate the use of language in written English.

Level: Intermediate to Advanced

Duration: 1 hour and 30 minutes

Materials Needed

- Sample song lyrics (printed or digital)
- Song Lyrics Analysis Checklist

Teaching Outline

Introduction (10 minutes)

Begin by discussing the importance of song lyrics in conveying messages, emotions, and stories. Explain that analyzing song lyrics involves examining the language, themes, poetic devices, and overall impact of the song. Encourage learners to share a song they find meaningful and discuss briefly why they like the lyrics.

Warm-Up (10 minutes)

Display examples of song lyrics. Read through them together and highlight various elements such as metaphors, similes, imagery, and themes. Discuss how these elements contribute to the overall meaning and emotional impact of the song.

Choosing a Song (10 minutes)

Ask learners to choose a song they enjoy or are curious about. Ensure that the song has rich lyrical content suitable for analysis. Provide some suggestions if needed, and ensure the lyrics are appropriate for the classroom setting.

Analyzing the Song Lyrics (20 minutes)

Distribute the Song Lyrics Analysis Checklist. Instruct learners to analyze their chosen song lyrics, focusing on the following:

- Identifying the main theme or message of the song
- Noting the use of poetic devices such as metaphors, similes, and imagery
- Examining the structure of the lyrics, including verses, chorus, and any repetition
- Interpreting the emotional tone and mood of the song
- Reflecting on the personal or cultural significance of the lyrics

Peer Discussion (10 minutes)

Have learners pair up and discuss their analyses with a partner. Encourage them to compare interpretations and discuss different perspectives on the same song or different songs. This will help them understand how lyrics can be interpreted in various ways.

Writing the Analysis (20 minutes)

Learners write a detailed analysis of their chosen song lyrics, incorporating their findings from the checklist and peer discussion. They should aim to explain the significance of the lyrics, how the poetic devices enhance the meaning, and their personal response to the song.

Reflection (10 minutes)

Conduct a class discussion on what they learned about analyzing song lyrics. Facilitate a reflective discussion where learners can articulate their insights and discoveries about the analysis process and how it deepened their appreciation of the song.

Song Lyrics Analysis Checklist

Theme

- What is the main theme or message of the song?
- How is this theme conveyed through the lyrics?

Poetic Devices

- Identify the metaphors, similes, and imagery used in the song.
- How do these poetic devices enhance the meaning and impact of the lyrics?

Structure

- Describe the structure of the lyrics (verses, chorus, repetition).
- How does the structure contribute to the overall flow and message of the song?

Emotional Tone and Mood

- What is the emotional tone and mood of the song?
- How do the lyrics convey these emotions?

Significance

- Reflect on the personal or cultural significance of the lyrics.
- Why do these lyrics resonate with you or the broader audience?

Assessment

Evaluate the learners' analyses based on the depth of interpretation, identification and explanation of poetic devices, understanding of the structure, and articulation of the emotional tone and significance. Consider how well they incorporated insights from the peer discussion and whether their analyses effectively convey a deeper understanding of the song lyrics.

This activity helps learners develop analytical skills, which are essential for interpreting and appreciating language in various forms. It enhances their ability to identify and explain poetic devices, understand themes and emotional tones, and articulate personal responses.

Book Review

Objective: Learners will practice writing detailed and engaging book reviews, improving their ability to summarize content, analyze themes, and express opinions in written English.

Level: Intermediate to Advanced

Duration: 1 hour and 30 minutes

Materials Needed

- Sample book reviews (printed or digital)
- Book Review Writing Checklist

Teaching Outline

Introduction (10 minutes)

Begin by discussing the purpose and importance of book reviews, such as helping readers decide whether to read a book and providing feedback to authors. Explain the key components of an effective book review: a brief summary of the book, analysis of key themes and characters, the reviewer's opinion, and a recommendation. Encourage learners to share their favorite books and discuss what they might include in a review.

Warm-Up (10 minutes)

Display examples of well-written book reviews. Highlight the different elements that make these reviews effective, such as a concise summary, insightful analysis, balanced opinions, and clear recommendations.

Discuss the importance of being honest and respectful while expressing opinions.

Choosing a Book (10 minutes)

Ask learners to choose a book they have recently read and feel strongly about. It can be a fiction or non-fiction book, as long as they can recall its key elements. Encourage them to take notes on the plot, themes, characters, and their personal reactions while they read.

Drafting the Book Review (20 minutes)

Distribute the Book Review Writing Checklist. Instruct learners to write their book review, ensuring they include:

- A brief summary that provides an overview of the plot without giving away spoilers
- An analysis of key themes, characters, and writing style
- Their personal opinion on the book, including strengths and weaknesses
- A recommendation for potential readers, stating who might enjoy the book and why

Peer Review (15 minutes)

Have learners exchange book reviews with a partner. Partners review each other's work using the Book Review Writing Checklist. Encourage learners to focus on the clarity and conciseness of the summary, the depth of the analysis, the balance and honesty of the opinions, and the persuasiveness of the recommendation.

Final Draft (15 minutes)

Learners revise their book reviews based on the feedback received. They then write the final draft of their review. Optionally, they can share their reviews in a small group or class discussion, simulating a book club or literary forum.

Reflection (10 minutes)

Conduct a class discussion on what they learned about writing book reviews. Facilitate a reflective discussion where learners can articulate their insights and discoveries about the review writing process and its importance in literary culture.

Book Review Writing Checklist

Summary

- Does the summary provide an overview of the plot without giving away spoilers?
- Is the summary concise and informative?

Analysis

- Are key themes and characters analyzed effectively?
- Is the writing style of the book discussed?

Opinion

- Is the reviewer's opinion clear and well-supported?
- Are both strengths and weaknesses of the book addressed?

Recommendation

- Is there a clear recommendation for potential readers?
- Does the recommendation specify who might enjoy the book and why?

Clarity and Honesty

- Is the review free of spelling and grammatical errors?
- Is the language clear and easy to understand?
- Is the reviewer's tone respectful and honest?

Assessment

Evaluate the learners' book reviews based on the clarity and conciseness of the summary, the depth and insight of the analysis, the balance and support of the opinion, and the effectiveness of the recommendation. Consider how well they incorporated feedback from the peer review and whether their reviews effectively engage and inform potential readers.

This activity helps learners develop critical thinking and analytical skills, which are essential for evaluating and discussing literature. It enhances their ability to summarize content concisely, analyze themes and characters, and express balanced and well-supported opinions.

ESL Writing Activities for Kids and Adults

Character Diary

Objective: Learners will practice creative writing by composing diary entries from the perspective of a fictional character, enhancing their ability to understand character development, voice, and perspective in written English.

Level: Intermediate to Advanced

Duration: 1 hour and 30 minutes

Materials Needed

- Sample diary entries from fictional characters (printed or digital)
- Character Diary Writing Checklist

Teaching Outline

Introduction (10 minutes)

Begin by discussing the purpose and value of diary entries, both in real life and fiction. Explain how writing diary entries can help explore a character's inner thoughts, feelings, and personal growth. Emphasize the importance of voice and perspective in making the character's diary authentic and engaging. Encourage learners to think about their favorite characters from books, movies, or TV shows and how those characters might express themselves in a diary.

Warm-Up (10 minutes)

Display examples of fictional diary entries. Highlight different elements that make these entries effective, such as a clear voice, vivid descriptions of events, and emotional depth. Discuss how the diary format allows for introspection and a deeper understanding of the character's motivations and experiences.

Choosing a Character (10 minutes)

Ask learners to choose a fictional character they are familiar with, from either a book, movie, or TV show. Alternatively, they can create their own character. Encourage them to take notes on the character's background, personality traits, significant events in their story, and their relationships with other characters.

Drafting the Diary Entry (20 minutes)

Distribute the Character Diary Writing Checklist. Instruct learners to write a diary entry from their chosen character's perspective, ensuring they include:

- A clear and authentic voice that reflects the character's personality
- Descriptions of recent events or experiences from the character's life
- The character's thoughts, feelings, and reactions to these events
- Reflections on relationships with other characters
- Insights into the character's personal growth or struggles

Peer Review (15 minutes)

Have learners exchange diary entries with a partner. Partners review each other's work using the Character Diary Writing Checklist. Encourage learners to focus on the authenticity of the voice, the vividness of the descriptions, the depth of the emotional content, and the clarity of the reflections.

Final Draft (15 minutes)

Learners revise their diary entries based on the feedback received. They then write the final draft of their diary entry. Optionally, they can share their entries in a small group or class discussion, allowing for further exploration of the characters' perspectives and development.

Reflection (10 minutes)

Conduct a class discussion on what they learned about writing diary entries from a character's perspective. Facilitate a reflective discussion where learners can articulate their insights and discoveries about character development, voice, and perspective.

Character Diary Writing Checklist

Voice

- Is the voice authentic and reflective of the character's personality?
- Does the writing style match the character's background and traits?

Descriptions

- Are recent events or experiences described engagingly?
- Do the descriptions help to paint a clear picture of the character's world?

Emotional Content

- Are the character's thoughts and feelings clearly conveyed?
- Does the diary entry provide emotional depth and insight?

Reflections

- Are the character's relationships with other characters explored?
- Does the entry include reflections on personal growth?

Clarity and Engagement

- Is the diary entry free of spelling and grammatical errors?
- Is the language clear and easy to understand?
- Is the diary entry engaging and does it hold the reader's interest?

Assessment

Evaluate the learners' diary entries based on the authenticity of the voice, the vividness of the descriptions, the depth and clarity of the emotional content, and the thoroughness of the reflections. Consider how well they incorporated feedback from the peer review and whether their entries effectively bring the character to life.

This activity helps learners develop creative writing skills, which are essential for exploring character development and perspective. It enhances their ability to write in an authentic voice, describe events vividly, and convey deep emotional content. The activity encourages empathy and understanding by putting learners in the shoes of a fictional character.

Podcast Script

Objective: Learners will practice writing a podcast script, improving their ability to organize content, convey information clearly, and engage an audience through spoken English.

Level: Intermediate to Advanced

Duration: 1 hour and 30 minutes

Materials Needed

- Sample podcast scripts or episodes (printed or digital)
- Podcast Script Writing Checklist

Teaching Outline

Introduction (10 minutes)

Begin by discussing the growing popularity of podcasts and their various formats, such as interviews, storytelling, news, and educational content. Explain the key elements of a successful podcast script: a clear structure, engaging content, natural dialogue, and audience interaction. Encourage learners to share their favorite podcasts and discuss what makes them engaging.

Warm-Up (10 minutes)

Play a short clip from a well-structured podcast. Highlight the elements that make it effective, such as a strong opening, clear organization, engaging dialogue, and a compelling closing. Discuss the importance of tone and pacing in maintaining listener interest.

Choosing a Topic (10 minutes)

Ask learners to choose a topic they are passionate about or knowledgeable in. This could range from hobbies and interests to current events and educational content. Encourage them to think about their target audience and what kind of content would be engaging and valuable to them.

Drafting the Podcast Script (20 minutes)

Distribute the Podcast Script Writing Checklist. Instruct learners to draft their podcast script, ensuring they include:

- A strong and engaging introduction that hooks the listener
- A clear structure that outlines the main points or segments
- Natural and conversational dialogue
- Interactive elements, such as questions or calls to action
- A compelling closing that summarizes the content and leaves a lasting impression

Peer Review (15 minutes)

Have learners exchange podcast scripts with a partner. Partners review each other's work using the Podcast Script Writing Checklist. Encourage learners to focus on the clarity of the structure, the engagement level of the content, the naturalness of the dialogue, and the effectiveness of the interactive elements.

Final Draft (15 minutes)

Learners revise their podcast scripts based on the feedback received. They then write the final draft of their script. Optionally, they can record a short segment of their podcast and share it with the class for additional feedback.

Reflection (10 minutes)

Conduct a class discussion on what they learned about writing podcast scripts. Facilitate a reflective discussion where learners can articulate their insights and discoveries about structuring content, engaging an audience, and the nuances of spoken English.

Podcast Script Writing Checklist

Introduction

- Does the introduction hook the listener?
- Is the purpose of the podcast clearly stated?

Structure

- Is there a clear outline of the main points or segments?
- Does the script flow logically from one segment to the next?

Dialogue

- Is the dialogue natural and conversational?
- Are technical terms and jargon explained for the audience?

Interactive Elements

- Are there questions or calls to action that engage the audience?
- Are listeners encouraged to interact or respond?

Closing

- Is the content summarized effectively?
- Does the closing leave a lasting impression?

Clarity and Engagement

- Is the script free of spelling and grammatical errors?
- Is the language clear and easy to understand?
- Is the content engaging and does it hold the listener's interest?

Assessment

Evaluate the learners' podcast scripts based on the clarity and engagement of the introduction, the logical flow and structure, the naturalness of the dialogue, the effectiveness of the interactive elements, and the strength of the closing. Consider how well they incorporated feedback from the peer review and whether their scripts effectively convey the intended content and engage the audience.

This activity helps learners develop skills in organizing content and writing for spoken delivery, which are essential for creating engaging and informative podcasts. It enhances their ability to structure information clearly, use conversational language, and interact with an audience.

News Report

Objective: Learners will practice writing a news report, improving their ability to summarize events, use journalistic language, and convey information clearly and objectively in written English.

Level: Intermediate to Advanced

Duration: 1 hour and 30 minutes

Materials Needed

- Sample news reports (printed or digital)
- News Report Writing Checklist

Teaching Outline

Introduction (10 minutes)

Begin by discussing the purpose of news reports and their role in informing the public about recent events. Explain the key elements of a news report: the headline, lead (opening paragraph), body, and conclusion. Emphasize the importance of clarity, objectivity, and factual accuracy. Encourage learners to share their favorite news sources and discuss what makes their reports reliable and engaging.

Warm-Up (10 minutes)

Display examples of well-written news reports. Highlight different elements that make these reports effective, such as a strong headline, a concise and informative lead, clear and organized body paragraphs, and a summarizing conclusion. Discuss the importance of the "5 Ws and 1 H" (Who, What, When, Where, Why, and How) in news reporting.

Choosing a Topic (10 minutes)

Ask learners to choose a recent event or topic that interests them. This could be a local community event, a national news story, or an international issue. Encourage them to conduct brief research to gather factual information and relevant details about the event.

Drafting the News Report (20 minutes)

Distribute the News Report Writing Checklist. Instruct learners to draft their news report, ensuring they include:

- A compelling headline that grabs the reader's attention
- A concise lead that summarizes the main points of the report
- Detailed body paragraphs that expand on the lead, providing context, quotes, and factual information
- A conclusion that summarizes the key points and provides any additional relevant information

Peer Review (15 minutes)

Have learners exchange news reports with a partner. Partners review each other's work using the News Report Writing Checklist. Encourage learners to focus on the effectiveness of the headline, the clarity and informativeness of the lead, the organization and detail of the body paragraphs, and the completeness of the conclusion.

Final Draft (15 minutes)

Learners revise their news reports based on the feedback received. They then write the final draft of their report. Optionally, they can present their news report to the class, simulating a news broadcast.

Reflection (10 minutes)

Conduct a class discussion on what they learned about writing news reports. Facilitate a reflective discussion where learners can articulate their insights and discoveries about journalistic writing, objectivity, and the importance of factual accuracy.

News Report Writing Checklist

Headline

- Is the headline compelling and attention-grabbing?
- Does it accurately reflect the content of the report?

Lead

- Does the lead summarize the main points of the report?
- Is the lead concise and informative?

Body

- Are the body paragraphs organized logically?
- Do they provide detailed and relevant information?
- Are quotes and factual information included to support the report?

Conclusion

- Does the conclusion summarize the key points effectively?
- Does it provide any additional relevant information?

Clarity and Objectivity

- Is the report free of spelling and grammatical errors?
- Is the language clear and easy to understand?
- Is the report objective and free of personal bias?

Assessment

Evaluate the learners' news reports based on the effectiveness of the headline, the clarity and informativeness of the lead, the organization and detail of the body paragraphs, and the completeness of the conclusion. Consider how well they incorporated feedback from the peer review and whether their reports effectively convey the event's details clearly and objectively.

This activity helps learners develop journalistic writing skills, which are essential for summarizing events and conveying information clearly and objectively. It enhances their ability to write concise leads, organize detailed information, maintain factual accuracy, and produce informative news reports for real-world contexts.

ESL Writing Activities for Kids and Adults

Travel Itinerary

Objective: Learners will practice writing a detailed travel itinerary, improving their ability to organize information, provide clear instructions, and engage an audience with descriptive language in written English.

Level: Intermediate to Advanced

Duration: 1 hour and 30 minutes

Materials Needed

- Sample travel itineraries (printed or digital)
- Travel Itinerary Writing Checklist

Teaching Outline

Introduction (10 minutes)

Begin by discussing the purpose and importance of travel itineraries. Explain how a well-organized itinerary helps travelers make the most of their trips by providing a clear plan of activities, accommodations, and transportation. Highlight the key elements of an effective travel itinerary: dates, destinations, activities, accommodations, and travel details. Encourage learners to share their own travel experiences and the importance of planning.

Warm-Up (10 minutes)

Display examples of detailed and engaging travel itineraries. Highlight different elements that make these itineraries effective, such as clear organization, detailed descriptions, practical information, and engaging language. Discuss how these elements help travelers visualize and prepare for their trips.

Choosing a Destination (10 minutes)

Ask learners to choose a destination they are interested in, whether it is a place they have visited before or a dream destination. Encourage them to research the destination briefly, gathering information about popular attractions, accommodations, transportation options, and local culture.

Drafting the Travel Itinerary (20 minutes)

Distribute the Travel Itinerary Writing Checklist. Instruct learners to draft their travel itinerary, ensuring they include:

- Clear and specific dates for the trip
- Detailed descriptions of daily activities and destinations
- Information about accommodations, including check-in/check-out times and amenities
- Transportation details, such as flights, trains, or car rentals, including departure and arrival times
- Practical information, such as local customs, weather forecasts, and packing tips

Peer Review (15 minutes)

Have learners exchange travel itineraries with a partner. Partners review each other's work using the Travel Itinerary Writing Checklist. Encourage learners to focus on the clarity and organization of the itinerary, the level of detail in the descriptions, and the practicality of the information provided.

Final Draft (15 minutes)

Learners revise their travel itineraries based on the feedback received. They then write the final draft of their itinerary. Optionally, they can present their itineraries to the class, simulating a travel agency pitch or a travel blog post.

Reflection (10 minutes)

Conduct a class discussion on what they learned about writing travel itineraries. Facilitate a reflective discussion where learners can articulate their insights and discoveries about organizing travel information, describing destinations, and providing practical travel advice.

Travel Itinerary Writing Checklist

Dates

- Are the dates for the trip clear and specific?
- Is the duration of the trip well-defined?

Daily Activities

- Are daily activities and destinations described in detail?
- Is the schedule realistic and manageable?

Accommodations

- Is information about accommodations clear and complete?
- Are check-in/check-out times and amenities included?

Transportation

- Are transportation details clear and specific?
- Are departure and arrival times included?

Practical Information

- Is practical information, such as local customs included?
- Are packing tips and other helpful advice provided?

Clarity and Organization

- Is the itinerary free of spelling and grammatical errors?
- Is the language clear and easy to understand?
- Is the itinerary well-organized and easy to follow?

Assessment

Evaluate the learners' travel itineraries based on the clarity and specificity of the dates, the detail and realism of the daily activities, the completeness of the accommodations and transportation details, and the usefulness of the practical information provided. Consider how well they incorporated feedback from the peer review and whether their itineraries effectively help travelers visualize and prepare for the trip.

This activity helps learners develop organizational and descriptive writing skills, which are essential for planning and communicating travel information. It enhances their ability to write clear and detailed itineraries, organize practical information, and engage an audience with descriptive language.

ESL Writing Activities for Kids and Adults

Speech Writing

Objective: Learners will practice writing a speech, improving their ability to organize ideas, use persuasive and engaging language, and deliver content clearly and confidently in spoken English.

Level: Intermediate to Advanced

Duration: 1 hour and 30 minutes

Materials Needed

- Sample speeches (printed or digital)
- Speech Writing Checklist

Teaching Outline

Introduction (10 minutes)

Begin by discussing the purpose and various contexts of speech writing, such as persuasive, informative, ceremonial, and special occasion speeches. Explain the key elements of an effective speech: a clear structure, engaging opening, well-organized body, and memorable conclusion. Emphasize the importance of understanding the audience and purpose when crafting a speech. Encourage learners to share any memorable speeches they've heard and discuss what made those speeches effective.

Warm-Up (10 minutes)

Display examples of effective speeches. Highlight different elements that make these speeches engaging, such as a strong opening, the use of anecdotes or statistics, clear organization, and a powerful conclusion. Discuss the importance of tone, pacing, and body language in delivering a speech.

Choosing a Topic (10 minutes)

Ask learners to choose a topic they are passionate about or an event they would like to address. This could be a current issue, a personal experience, or a subject they are knowledgeable about. Encourage them to think about the purpose of their speech and the audience they are addressing.

Drafting the Speech (20 minutes)

Distribute the Speech Writing Checklist. Instruct learners to draft their speech, ensuring they include:

- An engaging opening that captures the audience's attention
- A clear thesis or main idea
- Well-organized body paragraphs that support the thesis with evidence, examples, and anecdotes
- Transitions that connect ideas smoothly
- A memorable conclusion that reinforces the main idea and leaves a lasting impression

Peer Review (15 minutes)

Have learners exchange speeches with a partner. Partners review each other's work using the Speech Writing Checklist. Encourage learners to focus on the effectiveness of the opening, the clarity of the thesis, the organization and support of the body paragraphs, the smoothness of transitions, and the impact of the conclusion.

Final Draft (15 minutes)

Learners revise their speeches based on the feedback received. They then write the final draft of their speech. Optionally, they can practice delivering their speech to a small group or the class, focusing on tone, pacing, and body language.

Reflection (10 minutes)

Conduct a class discussion on what they learned about writing and delivering speeches. Facilitate a reflective discussion where learners can articulate their insights and discoveries about organizing ideas, engaging an audience, and using persuasive language.

Speech Writing Checklist

Opening

- Does the opening capture the audience's attention?
- Is the purpose of the speech clear from the beginning?

Thesis

- Is there a clear thesis or main idea?
- Does the thesis set the stage for the rest of the speech?

Body

- Are the body paragraphs well-organized and supportive of the thesis?
- Are evidence, examples, and anecdotes used effectively?
- Are transitions smooth and logical?

Conclusion

- Does the conclusion reinforce the main idea?
- Does it leave a lasting impression on the audience?

Clarity and Engagement

- Is the speech free of spelling and grammatical errors?
- Is the language clear and easy to understand?
- Is the speech engaging and does it hold the audience's interest?

Assessment

Evaluate the learners' speeches based on the effectiveness of the opening, the clarity of the thesis, the organization and support of the body paragraphs, the smoothness of transitions, and the impact of the conclusion. Consider how well they incorporated feedback from the peer review and whether their speeches effectively engage and persuade the audience.

This activity helps learners develop organizational and persuasive writing skills, which are essential for crafting and delivering effective speeches. It enhances their ability to write engaging openings, clear theses, well-supported body paragraphs, and memorable conclusions.

ESL Writing Activities for Kids and Adults

Problem-Solution Essay

Objective: Learners will practice writing a problem-solution essay to enhance their ability to identify a problem, analyze its causes and effects, propose solutions, and present their analysis clearly and effectively in written English.

Level: Intermediate to Advanced

Duration: 2 hours

Materials Needed

- Examples of problem-solution essays (printed or digital)
- Problem-Solution Essay Writing Checklist

Teaching Outline

Introduction (10 minutes)

Start by explaining the purpose and structure of a problem-solution essay. Highlight that these essays identify a specific problem, analyze its causes and effects, propose feasible solutions, and argue why these solutions are effective. Discuss the importance of a clear thesis statement, logical organization, and the use of evidence to support the proposed solutions.

Warm-Up (10 minutes)

Present examples of well-written problem-solution essays. Discuss their key elements, such as a strong introduction with a thesis statement, body paragraphs that clearly explain the problem and propose solutions, and a conclusion that summarizes the analysis and calls for action. Highlight the importance of using clear and concise language to explain the problem and the proposed solutions.

Choosing a Topic (10 minutes)

Ask learners to choose a topic they are interested in that has a clear problem and potential solutions. These could be related to social issues, environmental concerns, community challenges, personal experiences, etc. Ensure that learners choose topics with enough depth to analyze in detail.

Planning the Essay (15 minutes)

Distribute the Problem-Solution Essay Writing Checklist. Instruct learners to outline their essay, including the following sections:

- **Introduction:** Introduce the topic, describe the problem, and present a clear thesis statement.
- **Body Paragraphs:** Organize the body paragraphs to explain the problem in detail, analyze its causes and effects, and propose specific, actionable solutions. Use evidence and examples to support the analysis and the proposed solutions.
- **Conclusion:** Summarize the main points of the essay, restate the thesis in a new light, and call for action or further consideration.

Writing the Draft (25 minutes)

Learners write the first draft of their problem-solution essay based on their outline. Encourage them to focus on providing clear explanations of the problem and its causes, as well as detailed and feasible solutions. Remind them to maintain coherence and logical flow throughout the essay.

Peer Review (20 minutes)

Have learners exchange their essays with a partner. Partners review each other's work using the Problem-Solution Essay Writing Checklist. Encourage learners to provide constructive feedback on the clarity and coherence of the essay, the strength of the problem analysis, and the feasibility and effectiveness of the proposed solutions.

Final Draft (20 minutes)

Learners revise their essays based on the feedback received. They then write the final draft of their problem-solution essay, ensuring that it is well-organized, clearly written, and effectively analyzes the problem and proposes practical solutions. Optionally, they can share their essays with the class, practicing their presentation and communication skills.

Reflection (10 minutes)

Conduct a class discussion on what they learned about writing problem-solution essays. Facilitate a reflective discussion where learners can articulate their insights and discoveries about identifying and analyzing problems, proposing feasible solutions, and organizing essays effectively.

Problem-Solution Essay Writing Checklist

Introduction

- Does the introduction provide a clear overview of the problem?
- Is there a strong thesis statement that outlines the main points of the essay?

Body Paragraphs

- Are the problem and its causes clearly explained and well-supported with evidence and examples?
- Are the proposed solutions detailed, feasible, and well-supported?
- Is there a logical progression from one point to the next?
- Are transitions between paragraphs smooth and coherent?

Conclusion

- Does the conclusion summarize the main points of the essay?
- Is the thesis restated in a new light?
- Is there a clear call for action or further consideration?

Clarity and Accuracy

- Is the essay written in a clear and concise manner?
- Is the information accurate and free of errors?

Organization and Flow

- Is the essay well-organized and logically structured?
- Are transitions between sections smooth and coherent?

Assessment

Evaluate the learners' essays based on the clarity and accuracy of the introduction, the effectiveness and coherence of the body paragraphs, the relevance and clarity of the conclusion, and the overall organization and flow of the essay. Consider how well they incorporated feedback from the peer review and whether their essays effectively analyze the problem and propose practical solutions.

This activity helps learners develop critical thinking and persuasive writing skills, which are essential for addressing real-world problems. It enhances their ability to describe issues clearly, propose feasible solutions, and present logical arguments supported by evidence.

ESL Writing Activities for Kids and Adults

Interview Transcription

Objective: Learners will practice transcribing an interview, improving their ability to listen carefully, accurately capture spoken language in written form, and develop skills in editing for clarity and readability.

Level: Intermediate to Advanced

Duration: 2 hours

Materials Needed

- Audio or video recording of an interview
- Headphones
- Interview Transcription Checklist

Teaching Outline

Introduction (10 minutes)

Begin by discussing the purpose and importance of interview transcription. Explain how transcriptions are used in various fields such as journalism, research, and media. Highlight the key elements of an effective transcription: accuracy, completeness, clarity, and readability. Emphasize the importance of capturing the exact words spoken and making necessary edits for readability without altering the speaker's meaning.

Warm-Up (10 minutes)

Display examples of well-transcribed interviews. Highlight elements that make these transcriptions effective, such as accurate representation of spoken language, clear formatting, and appropriate use of punctuation and paragraphing. Discuss common challenges in transcription, such as dealing with unclear audio, accents, and overlapping speech.

Choosing an Interview (10 minutes)

Provide learners with a selection of audio or video interviews to choose from. Ensure the interviews are clear and appropriate for their level. Alternatively, if resources allow, learners can conduct their own interviews in pairs or small groups and record them for transcription.

Transcribing the Interview (25 minutes)

Distribute the Interview Transcription Checklist. Instruct learners to listen to the interview carefully and transcribe it verbatim. Encourage them to use headphones for better clarity and to pause and rewind the recording as needed. Emphasize the importance of capturing every word accurately, including fillers and pauses, while ensuring the transcription is readable.

Editing for Clarity (15 minutes)

Once the initial transcription is complete, instruct learners to review and edit their work for clarity and readability. This includes adding punctuation, breaking long sentences into smaller ones, and formatting the transcription into paragraphs. Encourage learners to maintain the original meaning and tone of the speakers while making the text easier to read.

Peer Review (20 minutes)

Have learners exchange transcriptions with a partner. Partners review each other's work using the Interview Transcription Checklist.

Encourage learners to focus on the accuracy of the transcription, the clarity of the language, and the effectiveness of the formatting.

Final Draft (20 minutes)

Learners revise their transcriptions based on the feedback received. They then write the final draft of their transcription. Optionally, they can present their transcriptions to the class, highlighting any interesting points from the interview.

Reflection (10 minutes)

Conduct a class discussion on what they learned about transcribing interviews. Facilitate a reflective discussion where learners can articulate their insights and discoveries about capturing spoken language, editing for readability, and the importance of accuracy in transcription.

Interview Transcription Checklist

Accuracy

- Is the transcription an accurate representation of the spoken language?
- Are all words, including fillers and pauses, captured correctly?

Completeness

- Is the entire interview transcribed?
- Are any inaudible parts marked clearly?

Clarity

- Is the transcription clear and easy to read?
- Is punctuation used correctly to enhance readability?

Formatting

- Is the transcription formatted into paragraphs appropriately?
- Are speaker changes clearly indicated?

Readability

- Does the transcription maintain the original meaning and tone of the speakers?
- Are long sentences broken into smaller, manageable ones?

Assessment

Evaluate the learners' transcriptions based on the accuracy of the captured spoken language, the completeness of the transcription, and the clarity and readability of the edited text. Consider how well they incorporated feedback from the peer review and whether their transcriptions effectively represent the interview.

This activity helps learners develop listening and writing skills, which are essential for accurately capturing and representing spoken language. It enhances their ability to transcribe interviews verbatim, edit for clarity and readability, and maintain the original meaning and tone of the speakers.

ESL Writing Activities for Kids and Adults

Personal Narrative

Objective: Learners will practice writing a personal narrative, improving their ability to tell a story from their own experiences, use descriptive language, and structure a coherent and engaging narrative.

Level: Intermediate to Advanced

Duration: 1 hour and 30 minutes

Materials Needed

- Sample personal narratives (printed or digital)
- Personal Narrative Writing Checklist

Teaching Outline

Introduction (10 minutes)

Begin by discussing the purpose and importance of personal narratives. Explain how personal narratives allow writers to share meaningful experiences, reflect on their personal growth, and connect with readers on an emotional level. Highlight the key elements of an effective personal narrative: a clear structure, engaging introduction, detailed descriptions, and a reflective conclusion. Encourage learners to think about significant events or moments in their lives that have had an impact on them.

Warm-Up (10 minutes)

Display examples of well-written personal narratives. Highlight elements that make these narratives effective, such as vivid descriptions, emotional resonance, and a clear narrative arc. Discuss how these elements help to engage the reader and convey the writer's personal experience.

Choosing a Topic (10 minutes)

Ask learners to brainstorm significant events or moments in their lives that they would like to write about. This could be a memorable trip, a challenging experience, a personal achievement, or a moment of realization. Encourage them to choose a topic that is meaningful to them and that they feel comfortable sharing.

Drafting the Narrative (20 minutes)

Distribute the Personal Narrative Writing Checklist. Instruct learners to draft their narrative, ensuring they include:

- An engaging introduction that sets the scene and introduces the main event or experience
- Detailed descriptions that use sensory language to bring the experience to life
- A clear narrative arc with a beginning, middle, and end
- Reflections on the significance of the experience and its impact on the writer

Peer Review (15 minutes)

Have learners exchange narratives with a partner. Partners review each other's work using the Personal Narrative Writing Checklist. Encourage learners to focus on the clarity and engagement of the introduction, the vividness of the descriptions, the coherence of the narrative arc, and the depth of the reflections.

Final Draft (15 minutes)

Learners revise their narratives based on the feedback received. They then write the final draft of their narrative. Optionally, they can share their narratives with the class, practicing their storytelling skills.

Reflection (10 minutes)

Conduct a class discussion on what they learned about writing personal narratives. Facilitate a reflective discussion where learners can articulate their insights and discoveries about sharing personal experiences, using descriptive language, and structuring a narrative.

ESL WRITING ACTIVITIES FOR KIDS AND ADULTS

Personal Narrative Writing Checklist

Introduction

- Does the introduction set the scene and introduce the main event or experience?
- Is the introduction engaging and does it capture the reader's attention?

Descriptions

- Are the descriptions detailed and vivid?
- Is sensory language used to bring the experience to life?

Narrative Arc

- Is there a clear beginning, middle, and end to the narrative?
- Is the sequence of events logical and easy to follow?

Reflections

- Does the narrative include reflections on the significance of the experience?
- Is the impact of the experience on the writer clearly conveyed?

Clarity and Engagement

- Is the narrative free of spelling and grammatical errors?
- Is the language clear and easy to understand?
- Is the narrative engaging and does it hold the reader's interest?

Assessment

Evaluate the learners' narratives based on the engagement and clarity of the introduction, the vividness and detail of the descriptions, the coherence and logic of the narrative arc, and the depth and clarity of the reflections. Consider how well they incorporated feedback from the peer review and whether their narratives effectively convey a meaningful personal experience.

This activity helps learners develop storytelling and descriptive writing skills, which are essential for sharing personal experiences and engaging readers. It enhances their ability to write vivid and detailed descriptions, structure a coherent narrative, and reflect on the significance of their experiences.

Annotated Bibliography

Objective: Learners will practice writing an annotated bibliography, improving their ability to summarize and evaluate sources, and organize research materials effectively in written English.

Level: Intermediate to Advanced

Duration: 1 hour and 30 minutes

Materials Needed

- Sample annotated bibliographies (printed or digital)
- Annotated Bibliography Writing Checklist

Teaching Outline

Introduction (10 minutes)

Begin by discussing the purpose and importance of an annotated bibliography. Explain how annotated bibliographies help researchers organize their sources, provide summaries, and critically evaluate the relevance and quality of each source. Highlight the key elements of an effective annotated bibliography: a citation, a summary of the source, and an evaluation of its relevance and quality. Encourage learners to think about how this tool can aid in their research projects.

Warm-Up (10 minutes)

Display examples of well-written annotated bibliographies. Highlight elements that make these annotations effective, such as concise summaries, critical evaluations, and proper citation format. Discuss the differences between descriptive and critical annotations and the importance of balancing summary with evaluation.

Choosing Sources (10 minutes)

Ask learners to choose a research topic they are interested in or working on for another class. Instruct them to find at least three sources related to their topic. These can include books, academic articles, reputable websites, and other relevant materials. Encourage them to evaluate the credibility and relevance of each source during their selection process.

Drafting Annotations (20 minutes)

Distribute the Annotated Bibliography Writing Checklist. Instruct learners to draft their annotations, ensuring they include:

- A complete and correctly formatted citation for each source
- A concise summary of the content and main arguments of the source
- An evaluation of the source's relevance, credibility, and quality
- An explanation of how the source will be useful in their research

Peer Review (15 minutes)

Have learners exchange annotated bibliographies with a partner. Partners review each other's work using the Annotated Bibliography Writing Checklist. Encourage learners to focus on the completeness and accuracy of the citations, the clarity and conciseness of the summaries, and the depth and insight of the evaluations.

Final Draft (15 minutes)

Learners revise their annotated bibliographies based on the feedback received. They then write the final draft of their annotations. Optionally, they can present their annotations to the class, explaining their research topic and the value of each source.

Reflection (10 minutes)

Conduct a class discussion on what they learned about writing annotated bibliographies. Facilitate a reflective discussion where learners can articulate their insights and discoveries about summarizing and evaluating sources, organizing research materials, and the importance of critical thinking in research.

Annotated Bibliography Writing Checklist

Citation

- Is the citation complete and correctly formatted?
- Does it follow the required citation style (e.g., APA, MLA, Chicago)?

Summary

- Is the summary concise and clear?
- Does it accurately reflect the main arguments and content of the source?

Evaluation

- Does the evaluation assess the relevance, credibility, and quality of the source?
- Does it explain how the source will be useful in the research?

Clarity and Organization

- Is the annotation free of spelling and grammatical errors?
- Is the language clear and easy to understand?
- Are the annotations well-organized and logically structured?

Assessment

Evaluate the learners' annotated bibliographies based on the completeness and accuracy of the citations, the clarity and conciseness of the summaries, and the depth and insight of the evaluations. Consider how well they incorporated feedback from the peer review and whether their annotations effectively organize and critique the sources.

This activity helps learners develop research and critical thinking skills, which are essential for organizing and evaluating sources. It enhances their ability to write clear and concise summaries, assess the relevance and quality of sources, and organize research materials effectively.

Debate Argument

Objective: Learners will practice writing a structured debate argument, improving their ability to construct logical arguments, present evidence, and engage in persuasive writing.

Level: Intermediate to Advanced

Duration: 1 hour and 30 minutes

Materials Needed

- Sample debate arguments (printed or digital)
- Debate Argument Writing Checklist

Teaching Outline

Introduction (10 minutes)

Begin by discussing the structure and purpose of a debate argument. Explain how debate arguments involve presenting a clear position on a topic, supporting it with evidence, and addressing potential counterarguments. Highlight the key elements: a clear thesis statement, supporting arguments, evidence, and a rebuttal to counterarguments. Emphasize the importance of logical reasoning and persuasive language in making an effective argument.

Warm-Up (10 minutes)

Display examples of well-written debate arguments. Highlight elements that make these arguments effective, such as a strong thesis, well-supported points, and a thorough consideration of counterarguments. Discuss the importance of using credible sources and logical reasoning to support their position.

Choosing a Topic (10 minutes)

Ask learners to choose a debate topic they are interested in. This could be a current event, a social issue, or a controversial topic. Encourage them to choose a topic that they feel passionate about and that has enough evidence available for both sides of the argument.

Drafting the Argument (20 minutes)

Distribute the Debate Argument Writing Checklist. Instruct learners to draft their debate argument, ensuring they include:

- A clear thesis statement that states their position on the topic
- At least three supporting arguments, each backed by credible evidence
- A consideration of at least one counterargument, along with a rebuttal

Peer Review (15 minutes)

Have learners exchange debate arguments with a partner. Partners review each other's work using the Debate Argument Writing Checklist. Encourage learners to focus on the clarity and strength of the thesis, the relevance and credibility of the supporting evidence, and the effectiveness of the rebuttal.

Final Draft (15 minutes)

Learners revise their debate arguments based on the feedback received. They then write the final draft of their argument. Optionally, they can present their arguments to the class, practicing their persuasive speaking skills.

Reflection (10 minutes)

Conduct a class discussion on what they learned about writing debate arguments. Facilitate a reflective discussion where learners can articulate their insights and discoveries about constructing logical arguments, using evidence effectively, and addressing counterarguments.

Debate Argument Writing Checklist

Thesis Statement

- Is the thesis statement clear and does it state the position on the topic?

Supporting Arguments

- Are there at least three supporting arguments?
- Is each argument backed by credible evidence?

Counterargument and Rebuttal

- Is at least one counterargument considered?
- Is the rebuttal logical and effective?

Clarity and Organization

- Is the argument free of spelling and grammatical errors?
- Is the language clear and persuasive?
- Is the argument well-organized and logically structured?

Assessment

Evaluate the learners' debate arguments based on the clarity and strength of the thesis, the relevance and credibility of the supporting evidence, and the effectiveness of the rebuttal. Consider how well they incorporated feedback from the peer review and whether their arguments effectively present a logical and persuasive case.

This activity helps learners develop critical thinking and persuasive writing skills, which are essential for constructing logical arguments and engaging in debates. It enhances their ability to present a clear thesis, support arguments with credible evidence, and address counterarguments.

ESL Writing Activities for Kids and Adults

Nature Description

Objective: Learners will practice writing detailed nature descriptions, improving their ability to use sensory language, create vivid imagery, and enhance their descriptive writing skills.

Level: Intermediate to Advanced

Duration: 1 hour and 30 minutes

Materials Needed

- Sample nature descriptions (printed or digital)
- Nature Description Writing Checklist

Teaching Outline

Introduction (10 minutes)

Begin by discussing the purpose and importance of descriptive writing, particularly in capturing the essence of natural settings. Explain how descriptive writing helps readers visualize scenes and experience the writer's observations through sensory language. Highlight the key elements of an effective nature description: vivid imagery, sensory details, and an organized structure. Encourage learners to think about their favorite natural settings and what makes those places special.

Warm-Up (10 minutes)

Display examples of well-written nature descriptions. Highlight elements that make these descriptions effective, such as the use of sensory language, detailed imagery, and a clear organizational structure.

Discuss how these elements help to immerse the reader in the described scene and convey the writer's experience of nature.

Choosing a Setting (10 minutes)

Ask learners to choose a natural setting they are familiar with or interested in describing. This could be a park, a beach, a forest, a mountain, or any other natural environment. Encourage them to think about the sensory details they can include, such as sights, sounds, smells, textures, and even tastes.

Drafting the Description (20 minutes)

Distribute the Nature Description Writing Checklist. Instruct learners to draft their nature description, ensuring they include:

- A clear introduction that sets the scene
- Detailed descriptions that use sensory language to create vivid imagery
- A logical organization that guides the reader through the scene
- Personal reflections or observations to add depth to the description

Peer Review (15 minutes)

Have learners exchange descriptions with a partner. Partners review each other's work using the Nature Description Writing Checklist. Encourage learners to focus on the vividness of the imagery, the effectiveness of the sensory language, and the overall organization and coherence of the description.

Final Draft (15 minutes)

Learners revise their descriptions based on the feedback received. They then write the final draft of their nature description. Optionally, they can share their descriptions with the class, practicing their descriptive writing and speaking skills.

Reflection (10 minutes)

Conduct a class discussion on what they learned about writing nature descriptions. Facilitate a reflective discussion where learners can articulate their insights and discoveries about using sensory language, creating vivid imagery, and organizing their descriptions.

ESL Writing Activities for Kids and Adults

Nature Description Writing Checklist

Introduction

- Does the introduction set the scene clearly?

Sensory Details

- Are detailed descriptions using sensory language included?
- Are sights, sounds, smells, textures, and tastes described effectively?

Imagery

- Does the writing create vivid imagery?
- Can the reader visualize the scene clearly?

Organization

- Is the description logically organized?
- Does it guide the reader through the scene?

Personal Reflections

- Are personal reflections or observations included?
- Do they add depth to the description?

Clarity and Organization

- Is the description free of spelling and grammatical errors?
- Is the language clear and descriptive?
- Is the description well-organized and logically structured?

Assessment

Evaluate the learners' nature descriptions based on the clarity of the introduction, the vividness and detail of the sensory descriptions, the effectiveness of the imagery, and the overall organization and coherence of the description. Consider how well they incorporated feedback from the peer review and whether their descriptions effectively convey the natural setting.

This activity helps learners develop descriptive writing skills, which are essential for creating vivid and engaging narratives. It enhances their ability to use sensory language, create detailed imagery, and organize descriptions logically. The activity encourages observation and reflection through the detailed depiction of natural settings.

… ESL Writing Activities for Kids and Adults

Business Proposal

Objective: Learners will practice writing a structured business proposal, improving their ability to present ideas clearly, use persuasive language, and structure formal business documents.

Level: Intermediate to Advanced

Duration: 1 hour and 30 minutes

Materials Needed

- Sample business proposals (printed or digital)
- Business Proposal Writing Checklist

Teaching Outline

Introduction (10 minutes)

Begin by discussing the purpose and importance of business proposals. Explain how business proposals are used to pitch ideas, request funding, or propose partnerships and how they must be clear, persuasive, and well-structured. Highlight the key elements of an effective business proposal: an executive summary, a detailed description of the project or idea, a market analysis, a financial plan, and a conclusion. Emphasize the importance of tailoring the proposal to the target audience.

Warm-Up (10 minutes)

Display examples of well-written business proposals. Highlight elements that make these proposals effective, such as a clear executive summary, detailed and feasible plans, thorough market analysis, and persuasive language. Discuss how these elements help to convince the reader of the viability and potential success of the proposed idea.

Choosing a Proposal Topic (10 minutes)

Ask learners to brainstorm and choose a business idea or project they are interested in proposing. This could be a new product, a service, a startup idea, or an improvement to an existing business process. Encourage them to choose an idea they are passionate about and that has potential market value.

Drafting the Proposal (20 minutes)

Distribute the Business Proposal Writing Checklist. Instruct learners to draft their business proposal, ensuring they include:

- An executive summary that provides a brief overview of the proposal
- A detailed description of the project or idea, including its goals and objectives
- A market analysis that identifies the target market and competition
- A financial plan that outlines the budget, projected costs, and potential revenue
- A conclusion that summarizes the key points and reiterates the proposal's value

Peer Review (15 minutes)

Have learners exchange proposals with a partner. Partners review each other's work using the Business Proposal Writing Checklist. Encourage learners to focus on the clarity and persuasiveness of the executive summary, the feasibility and detail of the project description, the thoroughness of the market analysis, and the accuracy and realism of the financial plan.

Final Draft (15 minutes)

Learners revise their proposals based on the feedback received. They then write the final draft of their business proposal. Optionally, they can present their proposals to the class, practicing their pitching and persuasive speaking skills.

Reflection (10 minutes)

Conduct a class discussion on what they learned about writing business proposals. Facilitate a reflective discussion where learners can articulate their insights and discoveries about presenting ideas clearly, using persuasive language, and structuring formal business documents.

Business Proposal Writing Checklist

Executive Summary

- Is the executive summary clear and does it provide a brief overview of the proposal?

Project Description

- Is the project or idea described in detail?
- Are the benefits and value of the project clearly outlined?

Market Analysis

- Is the target market identified?
- Is the competition analyzed thoroughly?

Financial Plan

- Is the budget clearly outlined?
- Are projected costs and potential revenue detailed and realistic?

Conclusion

- Does the conclusion summarize the key points?
- Does it reiterate the proposal's value persuasively?

Clarity and Organization

- Is the proposal free of spelling and grammatical errors?
- Is the language clear and persuasive?
- Is the proposal well-organized and logically structured?

Assessment

Evaluate the learners' business proposals based on the clarity and persuasiveness of the executive summary, the detail and feasibility of the project description, the thoroughness of the market analysis, the accuracy and realism of the financial plan, and the overall organization and coherence of the proposal. Consider how well they incorporated feedback from the peer review and whether their proposals effectively present and support their business ideas.

This activity helps learners develop formal writing and persuasive communication skills, which are essential for presenting business ideas and proposals. It enhances their ability to write clear and detailed descriptions, analyze markets, plan finances, and organize formal documents.

ESL Writing Activities for Kids and Adults

Formal Complaint

Objective: Learners will practice writing a formal complaint letter, improving their ability to communicate issues clearly and professionally, and to request appropriate resolutions.

Level: Intermediate to Advanced

Duration: 1 hour and 30 minutes

Materials Needed

- Sample formal complaint letters (printed or digital)
- Formal Complaint Letter Writing Checklist

Teaching Outline

Introduction (10 minutes)

Begin by discussing the purpose and importance of formal complaint letters. Explain how formal complaints are used to address issues, seek resolutions, and communicate dissatisfaction in a professional manner. Highlight the key elements of an effective formal complaint letter: a clear statement of the issue, specific details and evidence, a polite yet firm tone, and a request for a specific resolution. Emphasize the importance of maintaining professionalism throughout the letter.

Warm-Up (10 minutes)

Display examples of well-written formal complaint letters. Highlight elements that make these letters effective, such as a clear and concise description of the issue, relevant details and evidence, a polite tone, and a specific request for resolution. Discuss how these elements help to ensure the complaint is taken seriously and addressed appropriately.

Choosing a Complaint Topic (10 minutes)

Ask learners to think about a situation where they were dissatisfied with a product, service, or experience. This could be a recent personal experience or a hypothetical situation. Encourage them to choose a topic that they can describe in detail and for which they can think of a reasonable resolution.

Drafting the Letter (20 minutes)

Distribute the Formal Complaint Letter Writing Checklist. Instruct learners to draft their formal complaint letter, ensuring they include:

- A clear opening statement that identifies the purpose of the letter
- A detailed description of the issue, including specific details and any relevant evidence
- A polite yet firm tone throughout the letter
- A specific request for resolution or action to be taken
- Contact information for follow-up

Peer Review (15 minutes)

Have learners exchange letters with a partner. Partners review each other's work using the Formal Complaint Letter Writing Checklist. Encourage learners to focus on the clarity and specificity of the issue description, the appropriateness of the tone, and the feasibility of the requested resolution.

Final Draft (15 minutes)

Learners revise their letters based on the feedback received. They then write the final draft of their formal complaint letter. Optionally, they can read their letters to the class, practicing their formal writing and speaking skills.

Reflection (10 minutes)

Conduct a class discussion on what they learned about writing formal complaint letters. Facilitate a reflective discussion where learners can articulate their insights and discoveries about describing issues clearly, using a polite yet firm tone, and requesting specific resolutions.

Formal Complaint Letter Writing Checklist

Opening Statement

- Does the opening statement clearly identify the purpose of the letter?

Issue Description

- Is the issue described in detail?
- Are specific details and any relevant evidence included?

Tone

- Is the tone polite yet firm throughout the letter?
- Is professionalism maintained?

Resolution Request

- Is there a specific request for resolution or action to be taken?
- Is the requested resolution feasible?

Contact Information

- Is contact information provided for follow-up?

Clarity and Organization

- Is the letter free of spelling and grammatical errors?
- Is the language clear and concise?
- Is the letter well-organized and logically structured?

Assessment

Evaluate the learners' formal complaint letters based on the clarity and specificity of the issue description, the appropriateness and consistency of the tone, the feasibility of the requested resolution, and the overall organization and coherence of the letter. Consider how well they incorporated feedback from the peer review and whether their letters effectively communicate the complaint and request for resolution.

This activity helps learners develop formal writing and communication skills, which are essential for addressing issues and seeking resolutions in professional and personal contexts. It enhances their ability to describe issues clearly, use a polite yet firm tone, and request specific resolutions.

ESL Writing Activities for Kids and Adults

ESL WRITING ACTIVITIES FOR KIDS AND ADULTS

Short Story

Objective: Learners will practice writing a short story, improving their ability to create engaging narratives, develop characters, and use descriptive language to convey a plot and setting.

Level: Intermediate to Advanced

Duration: 1 hour and 30 minutes

Materials Needed

- Sample short stories (printed or digital)
- Short Story Writing Checklist

Teaching Outline

Introduction (10 minutes)

Begin by discussing the elements of a compelling short story: characters, setting, plot, conflict, and resolution. Explain how short stories are concise narratives that aim to engage the reader quickly and effectively. Highlight the importance of using descriptive language and vivid imagery to bring the story to life. Provide examples of how a short story can be structured and discuss different genres learners might explore.

Warm-Up (10 minutes)

Display examples of well-written short stories. Highlight elements that make these stories effective, such as strong character development, engaging plotlines, vivid descriptions, and satisfying resolutions.

Discuss how these elements work together to create an engaging and memorable narrative.

Choosing a Story Idea (10 minutes)

Ask learners to brainstorm ideas for their short stories. They can draw from personal experiences, imagine fictional scenarios, or be inspired by prompts. Encourage them to think about the genre they want to write in, such as mystery, romance, fantasy, or science fiction. Have them outline their main characters, setting, and basic plot.

Drafting the Story (20 minutes)

Distribute the Short Story Writing Checklist. Instruct learners to draft their short stories, ensuring they include:

- An engaging introduction that sets the scene and introduces the main characters
- A clear and compelling plot with a central conflict
- Detailed descriptions that use sensory language to create vivid imagery
- A resolution that provides closure to the story

Peer Review (15 minutes)

Have learners exchange stories with a partner. Partners review each other's work using the Short Story Writing Checklist. Encourage learners to focus on the clarity of the plot, the depth of the character development, the vividness of the descriptions, and the overall coherence and engagement of the narrative.

Final Draft (15 minutes)

Learners revise their stories based on the feedback received. They then write the final draft of their short story. Optionally, they can share their stories with the class, practicing their storytelling and descriptive writing skills.

Reflection (10 minutes)

Conduct a class discussion on what they learned about writing short stories. Facilitate a reflective discussion where learners can articulate their insights and discoveries about creating engaging narratives, developing characters, and using descriptive language.

Short Story Writing Checklist

Introduction

- Does the introduction set the scene and introduce the main characters?

Plot

- Is there a clear and compelling plot with a central conflict?

Descriptions

- Are detailed descriptions using sensory language included?
- Does the writing create vivid imagery?

Characters

- Are the characters well-developed and believable?
- Do the characters have clear motivations and growth?

Resolution

- Is there a resolution that provides closure to the story?
- Does the resolution tie up the main plot points effectively?

Clarity and Organization

- Is the story free of spelling and grammatical errors?
- Is the language clear and engaging?
- Is the story well-organized and logically structured?

Assessment

Evaluate the learners' short stories based on the clarity and engagement of the plot, the depth and believability of the characters, the vividness and detail of the descriptions, and the overall organization and coherence of the story. Consider how well they incorporated feedback from the peer review and whether their stories effectively convey an engaging narrative.

This activity helps learners develop creative writing and narrative skills, which are essential for crafting engaging and memorable stories. It enhances their ability to create vivid descriptions, develop believable characters, and structure coherent plots.

ESL Writing Activities for Kids and Adults

Memoir Excerpt

Objective: Learners will practice writing a memoir excerpt, improving their ability to narrate personal experiences, use reflective language, and engage readers with authentic storytelling.

Level: Intermediate to Advanced

Duration: 1 hour and 30 minutes

Materials Needed

- Sample memoir excerpts (printed or digital)
- Memoir Excerpt Writing Checklist

Teaching Outline

Introduction (10 minutes)

Begin by discussing the purpose and elements of a memoir. Explain how a memoir differs from an autobiography by focusing on specific, impactful moments or themes in the writer's life rather than a chronological account. Highlight the importance of reflective language, vivid descriptions, and emotional honesty in memoir writing. Provide examples of powerful memoir excerpts and discuss what makes them compelling.

Warm-Up (10 minutes)

Display examples of well-written memoir excerpts. Highlight elements that make these excerpts effective, such as the use of vivid imagery, deep reflection, and emotional resonance. Discuss how these elements help to engage the reader and convey the significance of the writer's experiences.

Choosing a Memoir Topic (10 minutes)

Ask learners to brainstorm significant moments or themes in their lives that they would like to write about. This could be a memorable event, a challenging experience, or a period of personal growth. Encourage them to choose a topic that they feel comfortable sharing and that has had a meaningful impact on their lives.

Drafting the Excerpt (20 minutes)

Distribute the Memoir Excerpt Writing Checklist. Instruct learners to draft their memoir excerpt, ensuring they include:

- A captivating opening that draws the reader into the experience
- Detailed descriptions that use sensory language to create vivid imagery
- Reflective language that explores the significance of the experience
- Emotional honesty that conveys the writer's true feelings and insights

Peer Review (15 minutes)

Have learners exchange excerpts with a partner. Partners review each other's work using the Memoir Excerpt Writing Checklist. Encourage learners to focus on the vividness of the descriptions, the depth of the reflection, and the emotional honesty of the writing.

Final Draft (15 minutes)

Learners revise their excerpts based on the feedback received. They then write the final draft of their memoir excerpt. Optionally, they can share their excerpts with the class, practicing their narrative and reflective writing skills.

Reflection (10 minutes)

Conduct a class discussion on what they learned about writing memoirs. Facilitate a reflective discussion where learners can articulate their insights and discoveries about narrating personal experiences, using reflective language, and engaging readers emotionally.

Memoir Excerpt Writing Checklist

Opening

- Does the opening draw the reader into the experience?

Descriptions

- Are detailed descriptions using sensory language included?
- Does the writing create vivid imagery?

Reflection

- Is reflective language used to explore the significance of the experience?
- Does the reflection add depth to the narrative?

Emotional Honesty

- Is the writing emotionally honest?
- Does it convey the writer's true feelings and insights?

Clarity and Organization

- Is the excerpt free of spelling and grammatical errors?
- Is the language clear and engaging?
- Is the excerpt well-organized and logically structured?

Assessment

Evaluate the learners' memoir excerpts based on the vividness and detail of the descriptions, the depth and insightfulness of the reflection, the emotional honesty of the writing, and the overall organization and coherence of the excerpt. Consider how well they incorporated feedback from the peer review and whether their excerpts effectively engage the reader and convey the significance of their experiences.

This activity helps learners develop narrative and reflective writing skills, which are essential for telling compelling personal stories. It enhances their ability to create vivid descriptions, explore the significance of their experiences, and convey emotions.

ESL Writing Activities for Kids and Adults

Photo Essay

Objective: Learners will practice creating a photo essay, improving their ability to combine visual and written elements to tell a compelling story or convey a specific message.

Level: Intermediate to Advanced

Duration: 2 hours

Materials Needed

- Digital cameras or smartphones
- Sample photo essays (printed or digital)
- Photo Essay Writing Checklist

Teaching Outline

Introduction (10 minutes)

Begin by discussing the concept and purpose of a photo essay. Explain how photo essays use a series of images, combined with written text, to tell a story or convey a message. Highlight the importance of choosing a central theme or topic, selecting powerful images, and writing captions or accompanying text that enhance the overall narrative. Provide examples of compelling photo essays and discuss the elements that make them effective.

Warm-Up (10 minutes)

Display examples of well-crafted photo essays. Highlight elements that make these photo essays effective, such as a clear and cohesive theme, powerful and well-composed images, and descriptive text that adds context and depth. Discuss how the combination of visual and written elements can create a more engaging and impactful story.

Choosing a Topic and Planning (10 minutes)

Ask learners to brainstorm topics or themes for their photo essays. This could be a day in their life, a local event, a social issue, or a personal journey. Encourage them to choose a topic that they are passionate about and that lends itself to visual storytelling. Have them plan the sequence of their photo essay, including the key images they want to capture and the accompanying text for each image.

Capturing Photos (30 minutes)

Learners go out and capture the images for their photo essays. Depending on the context, they can take photos in and around the classroom, on the school grounds, or in their local community. Encourage them to take a variety of shots, including wide angles, close-ups, and detailed images that support their chosen theme. Remind them to consider composition, lighting, and focus to ensure their images are clear and impactful.

Writing Accompanying Text (20 minutes)

Distribute the Photo Essay Writing Checklist. Instruct learners to write captions or short paragraphs to accompany each photo. These texts should provide context, explain the significance of the image, and contribute to the overall narrative of the photo essay. Encourage learners to be descriptive and to connect the text with the visual elements effectively.

Peer Review (15 minutes)

Have learners exchange photo essays with a partner. Partners review each other's work using the Photo Essay Writing Checklist. Encourage learners to focus on the coherence of the theme, the quality and relevance of the images, and the effectiveness of the accompanying text in enhancing the overall narrative.

Final Draft (15 minutes)

Learners revise their photo essays based on the feedback received. They then create the final version of their photo essay, ensuring that the images and text work together cohesively to tell a compelling story. Optionally, they can present their photo essays to the class, practicing their visual and written storytelling skills.

Reflection (10 minutes)

Conduct a class discussion on what they learned about creating photo essays. Facilitate a reflective discussion where learners can articulate their insights and discoveries about combining visual and written elements to tell a story, choosing impactful images, and writing descriptive text.

ESL Writing Activities for Kids and Adults

Photo Essay Writing Checklist

Theme and Narrative

- Is there a clear and cohesive theme or topic throughout the photo essay?
- Does the narrative effectively convey a story or message?

Images

- Are the images clear, well-composed, and impactful?
- Do the images support and enhance the theme or narrative?

Accompanying Text

- Does the text provide context and explain the significance of each image?
- Is the text descriptive and well-written?

Coherence

- Do the images and text work together cohesively to tell a compelling story?
- Is the photo essay logically sequenced and easy to follow?

Clarity and Organization

- Is the photo essay free of spelling and grammatical errors?
- Is the overall presentation clear and organized?

Assessment

Evaluate the learners' photo essays based on the clarity and coherence of the theme, the quality and relevance of the images, the descriptiveness and effectiveness of the accompanying text, and the overall organization and impact of the photo essay. Consider how well they incorporated feedback from the peer review and whether their photo essays effectively combine visual and written elements to convey a story or message.

This activity helps learners develop visual and written storytelling skills, which are essential for creating engaging and impactful narratives. It enhances their ability to choose and compose powerful images, write descriptive and contextual text, and combine visual and written elements effectively.

ESL Writing Activities for Kids and Adults

Editorial Cartoon Analysis

Objective: Learners will practice analyzing editorial cartoons, improving their ability to interpret visual rhetoric, understand underlying messages, and articulate their analysis in written form.

Level: Intermediate to Advanced

Duration: 1 hour and 30 minutes

Materials Needed

- Sample editorial cartoons (printed or digital)
- Editorial Cartoon Analysis Checklist

Teaching Outline

Introduction (10 minutes)

Begin by discussing the purpose and elements of editorial cartoons. Explain how editorial cartoons use imagery and humor to comment on social, political, and cultural issues. Highlight the importance of understanding symbolism, exaggeration, labeling, analogy, and irony in interpreting these cartoons. Provide examples of editorial cartoons and discuss their key elements and underlying messages.

Warm-Up (10 minutes)

Display examples of well-crafted editorial cartoons. Highlight elements that make these cartoons effective, such as the use of symbolism, exaggeration, and irony. Discuss how these elements help to convey the cartoonist's message and provoke thought or criticism about the depicted issue. Encourage learners to consider the cartoonist's perspective and the context in which the cartoon was created.

Choosing a Cartoon (10 minutes)

Ask learners to choose an editorial cartoon to analyze. This could be a cartoon related to a current event, historical event, or social issue. Encourage them to select a cartoon that interests them and that they feel confident interpreting. Provide access to a range of cartoons from different sources.

Analyzing the Cartoon (20 minutes)

Distribute the Editorial Cartoon Analysis Checklist. Instruct learners to analyze their chosen cartoon, considering the following aspects:

- **Symbolism**: What symbols are used in the cartoon, and what do they represent?
- **Exaggeration**: How are certain features exaggerated, and why?
- **Labeling**: Are there any labels used in the cartoon, and what is their significance?
- **Analogy**: What comparisons are made in the cartoon, and how do they enhance the message?
- **Irony**: Is there any irony present, and how does it contribute to the overall message?
- **Context**: What is the context in which the cartoon was created, and how does it influence its meaning?

Writing the Analysis (20 minutes)

Instruct learners to write a detailed analysis of their chosen cartoon, using their notes from the checklist. They should provide a clear interpretation of the cartoon's message, discuss the effectiveness of the visual elements, and consider the cartoonist's perspective and context.

Encourage them to support their analysis with specific examples from the cartoon.

Peer Review (15 minutes)

Have learners exchange analyses with a partner. Partners review each other's work using the Editorial Cartoon Analysis Checklist. Encourage learners to focus on the clarity of the interpretation, the depth of the analysis, and the effectiveness of the writing.

Final Draft (15 minutes)

Learners revise their analyses based on the feedback received. They then write the final draft of their editorial cartoon analysis. Optionally, they can share their analyses with the class, practicing their analytical and writing skills.

Reflection (10 minutes)

Conduct a class discussion on what they learned about analyzing editorial cartoons. Facilitate a reflective discussion where learners can articulate their insights and discoveries about interpreting visual rhetoric, understanding underlying messages, and writing analytical essays.

Editorial Cartoon Analysis Checklist

Symbolism

- Are the symbols identified with their meanings explained?

Exaggeration

- Are the exaggerated features identified and discussed?

Labeling

- Are the labels in the cartoon identified and explained?

Analogy

- Are the comparisons identified and their effects discussed?

Irony

- Is the irony in the cartoon identified and its contribution to the message analyzed?

Context

- Is the context of the cartoon explained and its influence on the meaning discussed?

Clarity and Organization

- Is the analysis free of spelling and grammatical errors?
- Is the language clear and engaging?
- Is the analysis well-organized and logically structured?

Assessment

Evaluate the learners' editorial cartoon analyses based on the clarity and depth of their interpretation, the effectiveness of their discussion of visual elements, the insightfulness of their context analysis, and the overall organization and coherence of their writing. Consider how well they incorporated feedback from the peer review and whether their analyses effectively convey an understanding of the cartoon's message and techniques.

This activity helps learners develop analytical and interpretive skills, which are essential for understanding visual rhetoric and underlying messages in editorial cartoons. It enhances their ability to identify and discuss symbolism, exaggeration, labeling, analogy, and irony.

ESL Writing Activities for Kids and Adults

Formal Report

Objective: Learners will practice writing a formal report, improving their ability to structure information, present data and findings clearly, and use formal language appropriate for academic or professional contexts.

Level: Intermediate to Advanced

Duration: 2 hours

Materials Needed

- Sample formal reports (printed or digital)
- Formal Report Writing Checklist

Teaching Outline

Introduction (10 minutes)

Begin by discussing the purpose and elements of a formal report. Explain how formal reports are used to convey information, present findings, and make recommendations based on data or research. Highlight the importance of a clear structure, formal language, and accurate data presentation. Provide examples of formal reports and discuss their key sections and purposes.

Warm-Up (10 minutes)

Display examples of well-written formal reports. Highlight elements that make these reports effective, such as a clear introduction, well-organized body, detailed findings, and concise conclusions.

Discuss how these elements help to convey information clearly and professionally. Emphasize the importance of using formal language and proper formatting.

Choosing a Topic (10 minutes)

Ask learners to choose a topic for their formal report. This could be a research topic, a business analysis, a scientific study, or any subject that requires a structured presentation of information. Encourage them to select a topic that interests them and that they have enough information or data to write about.

Planning the Report (15 minutes)

Distribute the Formal Report Writing Checklist. Instruct learners to outline their reports, including the following sections:

- **Title Page**: Includes the report title, author's name, date, and any other relevant information.
- **Abstract**: A brief summary of the report's contents.
- **Introduction**: Provides background information and states the report's purpose and objectives.
- **Methodology**: Describes the methods used to gather data or conduct research.
- **Findings/Results**: Presents the data or research findings in a clear and organized manner.
- **Discussion**: Analyzes and interprets the findings, discussing their implications.
- **Conclusion**: Summarizes the main points and may include recommendations based on the findings.
- **References**: Lists the sources used in the report.

Writing the Draft (25 minutes)

Learners write the first draft of their formal report based on their outline. Encourage them to focus on clarity, coherence, and formal language. Remind them to use headings and subheadings to organize their content and to present data in tables, graphs, or charts as appropriate.

Peer Review (20 minutes)

Have learners exchange reports with a partner. Partners review each other's work using the Formal Report Writing Checklist. Encourage learners to focus on the clarity of the structure, the accuracy and presentation of the data, the coherence of the analysis, and the use of formal language.

Final Draft (20 minutes)

Learners revise their reports based on the feedback received. They then write the final draft of their formal report, ensuring that it is well-organized, clearly written, and properly formatted. Optionally, they can present their reports to the class, practicing their presentation and formal writing skills.

Reflection (10 minutes)

Conduct a class discussion on what they learned about writing formal reports. Facilitate a reflective discussion where learners can articulate their insights and discoveries about structuring information, presenting data, and using formal language.

Formal Report Writing Checklist

Title Page

- Does the title page include the report title, author's name, date, and other relevant information?

Abstract

- Is the abstract a brief summary of the report's contents?

Introduction

- Does the introduction provide background information and state the report's purpose and objectives?

Methodology

- Is the methodology clearly described, explaining how data was gathered or research conducted?

Findings/Results

- Are the findings/results presented clearly and organized logically?
- Are tables, graphs, or charts used effectively to present data?

Discussion

- Does the discussion analyze and interpret the findings?
- Are the implications of the findings discussed?

Conclusion

- Does the conclusion summarize the main points?
- Are any recommendations based on the findings included?

References

- Are all sources used in the report listed properly?
- Is the referencing format consistent and correct?

Clarity and Organization

- Is the report free of spelling and grammatical errors?
- Is the language clear and formal?
- Is the report well-organized with appropriate headings and subheadings?

Assessment

Evaluate the learners' formal reports based on the clarity and coherence of the structure, the accuracy and presentation of the data, the depth of the analysis, the appropriateness of the conclusions and recommendations, and the use of formal language. Consider how well they incorporated feedback from the peer review and whether their reports effectively convey information in a structured and professional manner.

This activity helps learners develop skills in writing formal reports, which are essential for academic and professional communication. It enhances their ability to structure information clearly, present data accurately, and use formal language.

ESL Writing Activities for Kids and Adults

Story Continuation

Objective: Learners will practice creative writing by continuing a given story, enhancing their ability to develop plot, characters, and setting while maintaining coherence with the original text.

Level: Intermediate to Advanced

Duration: 1 hour and 30 minutes

Materials Needed

- A selection of story beginnings (printed or digital)
- Story Continuation Writing Checklist

Teaching Outline

Introduction (10 minutes)

Begin by discussing the concept and purpose of story continuation. Explain how this activity allows learners to exercise their creativity while also developing their ability to write cohesively with an existing narrative. Highlight the importance of maintaining the original tone, style, and character voices while adding new elements to the story.

Warm-Up (10 minutes)

Display examples of story beginnings. Read a few examples aloud and discuss potential directions the stories could take. Highlight how different choices in plot development, character actions, and settings can lead to unique and interesting continuations. Encourage learners to think creatively and consider multiple possibilities.

ESL Writing Activities for Kids and Adults

Choosing a Story Beginning (10 minutes)

Ask learners to choose a story beginning from the provided selection. Ensure that each story beginning is engaging and provides enough context for learners to build upon. Encourage them to select a story that sparks their interest and imagination.

Planning the Continuation (15 minutes)

Distribute the Story Continuation Writing Checklist. Instruct learners to brainstorm ideas for continuing their chosen story. They should consider the following aspects:

- **Plot Development**: What will happen next in the story? What conflicts or challenges will the characters face?
- **Character Development**: How will the characters grow or change? What new characters might be introduced?
- **Setting**: Where will the story take place? Will new settings be introduced?
- **Tone and Style**: How will they maintain the original tone and style of the story?

Writing the Continuation (25 minutes)

Learners write the continuation of their chosen story, using their brainstormed ideas as a guide. Encourage them to focus on creating a coherent and engaging narrative that flows naturally from the story beginning. Remind them to pay attention to details, such as character actions, dialogue, and setting descriptions.

Peer Review (20 minutes)

Have learners exchange their story continuations with a partner. Partners review each other's work using the Story Continuation Writing Checklist. Encourage learners to provide constructive feedback on plot coherence, character development, and adherence to the original tone and style.

Final Draft (20 minutes)

Learners revise their story continuations based on the feedback received. They then write the final draft of their continuation, ensuring that it is well-developed, coherent, and engaging. Optionally, they can share their continuations with the class, practicing their storytelling and presentation skills.

Reflection (10 minutes)

Conduct a class discussion on what they learned about continuing a story. Facilitate a reflective discussion where learners can articulate their insights and discoveries about plot development, character growth, and maintaining coherence with an existing narrative.

Story Continuation Writing Checklist

Plot Development

- Does the continuation logically follow from the beginning?
- Are new events and conflicts engaging?

Character Development

- Are the characters' voices and personalities maintained?
- Are new characters introduced in an interesting way?

Setting

- Is the original setting expanded or developed further?
- Are new settings introduced clearly and descriptively?

Tone and Style

- Is the original tone of the story maintained?
- Does the writing style remain consistent with the beginning?

Coherence and Flow

- Does the continuation flow naturally from the original story?
- Are transitions between events and scenes smooth?

Clarity and Organization

- Is the continuation free of spelling and grammatical errors?
- Is the language clear and engaging?
- Is the continuation well-organized and logically structured?

Assessment

Evaluate the learners' story continuations based on the coherence and creativity of the plot development, the depth of character development, the clarity and descriptiveness of the setting, the consistency of tone and style, and the overall organization and flow of the narrative. Consider how well they incorporated feedback from the peer review and whether their continuations effectively build upon the original story beginning.

This activity helps learners develop creative writing skills, which are essential for crafting engaging and coherent narratives. It enhances their ability to develop plot and characters, maintain tone and style consistency, and create seamless transitions.

ESL Writing Activities for Kids and Adults

ESL Writing Activities for Kids and Adults

Literary Analysis

Objective: Learners will practice writing a literary analysis, improving their ability to interpret and critique literary texts, develop thesis statements, and support their arguments with textual evidence.

Level: Intermediate to Advanced

Duration: 2 hours

Materials Needed

- A selection of literary texts (printed or digital)
- Literary Analysis Writing Checklist

Teaching Outline

Introduction (10 minutes)

Begin by discussing the purpose and elements of literary analysis. Explain how literary analysis involves examining the themes, characters, plot, and literary devices used in a text to understand its deeper meanings and significance. Highlight the importance of developing a clear thesis statement and supporting it with textual evidence.

Warm-Up (10 minutes)

Display examples of literary texts. Read a short passage from one of the texts aloud and discuss its key elements. Highlight how different literary devices, such as symbolism, metaphor, and imagery, contribute to the overall meaning of the text. Encourage learners to think critically about the text and to consider different interpretations.

Choosing a Text (10 minutes)

Ask learners to choose a literary text from the provided selection. Ensure that each text is rich in literary elements and offers ample material for analysis. Encourage them to select a text that interests them and that they feel confident analyzing.

Planning the Analysis (15 minutes)

Distribute the Literary Analysis Writing Checklist. Instruct learners to outline their analysis, including the following aspects:

- **Thesis Statement**: What is the main argument or interpretation of the text?
- **Introduction**: Provides background information about the text and states the thesis.
- **Body Paragraphs**: Each paragraph should focus on a specific aspect of the text (e.g., a theme, character, or literary device) and provide evidence to support the thesis.
- **Conclusion**: Summarizes the main points and restates the thesis in a new light.

Writing the Draft (25 minutes)

Learners write the first draft of their literary analysis based on their outline. Encourage them to focus on developing a clear thesis and supporting it with specific examples and quotations from the text. Remind them to analyze the text critically, discussing not just what happens, but why it happens and what it means.

Peer Review (20 minutes)

Have learners exchange their analyses with a partner. Partners review each other's work using the Literary Analysis Writing Checklist. Encourage learners to focus on the clarity of the thesis, the effectiveness of the supporting evidence, and the coherence and organization of the analysis.

Final Draft (20 minutes)

Learners revise their analyses based on the feedback received. They then write the final draft of their literary analysis, ensuring that it is well-organized, clearly written, and properly formatted. Optionally, they can share their analyses with the class, practicing their analytical and writing skills.

Reflection (10 minutes)

Conduct a class discussion on what they learned about writing literary analysis. Facilitate a reflective discussion where learners can articulate their insights and discoveries about interpreting literary texts, developing arguments, and supporting their analyses with textual evidence.

Literary Analysis Writing Checklist

Thesis Statement

- Is the thesis statement clear and specific?
- Does the thesis statement present a unique interpretation or argument?

Introduction

- Does the introduction provide relevant background information about the text?
- Does the introduction clearly state the thesis?

Body Paragraphs

- Does each paragraph focus on a specific aspect of the text?
- Are textual evidence and quotations used effectively to support the thesis?
- Are literary devices and their significance discussed in detail?

Conclusion

- Does the conclusion summarize the main points of the analysis?
- Does the conclusion restate the thesis in a new light?

Clarity and Organization

- Is the analysis free of spelling and grammatical errors?
- Is the language clear and engaging?
- Is the analysis well-organized and logically structured?

Assessment

Evaluate the learners' literary analyses based on the clarity and originality of the thesis statement, the effectiveness of the supporting evidence, the depth of the analysis, the coherence and organization of the essay, and the use of formal language. Consider how well they incorporated feedback from the peer review and whether their analyses effectively interpret and critique the literary text.

This activity helps learners develop critical thinking and analytical writing skills, which are essential for interpreting and critiquing literary texts. It enhances their ability to develop and support a thesis, use textual evidence effectively, and write coherently and persuasively.

Biography

Objective: Learners will practice writing a biography, improving their ability to research, organize information, and write about a person's life in a coherent and engaging manner.

Level: Intermediate to Advanced

Duration: 2 hours

Materials Needed

- Sample biographies (printed or digital)
- Biography Writing Checklist

Teaching Outline

Introduction (10 minutes)

Begin by discussing the purpose and elements of a biography. Explain how biographies are written accounts of a person's life, focusing on their achievements, challenges, and significant events. Highlight the importance of conducting thorough research, organizing information logically, and writing in a clear and engaging manner.

Warm-Up (10 minutes)

Display examples of well-written biographies. Read a short excerpt from one of the biographies aloud and discuss its key elements. Highlight how the biography provides a detailed account of the person's life, including their background, major accomplishments, and impact. Encourage learners to think about what makes a biography engaging.

ESL Writing Activities for Kids and Adults

Choosing a Subject (10 minutes)

Ask learners to choose a person they want to write a biography about. This could be a historical figure, a contemporary personality, a family member, or someone they admire. Ensure that learners choose someone they are interested in and can find sufficient information about.

Researching the Subject (10 minutes)

Distribute the Biography Writing Checklist. Instruct learners to conduct research on their chosen subject, gathering information about their background, early life, major achievements, challenges, and significant events. Encourage learners to use reliable sources, such as books, articles, and reputable websites, and to take detailed notes.

Planning the Biography (15 minutes)

Learners outline their biography, including the following sections:

- **Introduction**: Introduces the subject and provides an overview of their significance.
- **Early Life**: Describes the subject's background and early experiences.
- **Major Achievements**: Highlights the subject's key accomplishments and contributions.
- **Challenges and Struggles**: Discusses any difficulties or obstacles the subject faced.
- **Later Life and Legacy**: Covers the subject's later years and their lasting impact.

Writing the Draft (25 minutes)

Learners write the first draft of their biography based on their outline. Encourage them to focus on creating a coherent and engaging narrative that accurately reflects the subject's life and achievements. Remind them to use a mix of factual information and descriptive details to bring the biography to life.

Peer Review (15 minutes)

Have learners exchange their biographies with a partner. Partners review each other's work using the Biography Writing Checklist. Encourage learners to provide constructive feedback on the clarity, coherence, engagement, and accuracy of the information.

Final Draft (15 minutes)

Learners revise their biographies based on the feedback received. They then write the final draft of their biography, ensuring that it is well-organized, clearly written, and properly formatted. Optionally, they can share their biographies with the class, practicing their presentation and writing skills.

Reflection (10 minutes)

Conduct a class discussion on what they learned about writing biographies. Facilitate a reflective discussion where learners can articulate their insights and discoveries about researching, organizing, and writing about a person's life.

Biography Writing Checklist

Introduction

- Does the introduction effectively introduce the subject and provide an overview of their significance?

Early Life

- Does the biography provide detailed information about the subject's background and early experiences?

Major Achievements

- Are the subject's key accomplishments and contributions highlighted clearly and accurately?

Challenges and Struggles

- Are any difficulties or obstacles the subject faced discussed in detail?

Later Life and Legacy

- Does the biography cover the subject's later years and their lasting impact?

Clarity and Engagement

- Is the biography written in a clear and engaging manner?
- Are factual information and descriptive details used effectively to bring the biography to life?

Organization and Structure

- Is the biography well-organized and logically structured?

- Are transitions between sections smooth and coherent?

Clarity and Organization

- Is the biography free of spelling and grammatical errors?
- Is the language clear and engaging?
- Is the biography well-organized and logically structured?

Assessment

Evaluate the learners' biographies based on the clarity and engagement of the narrative, the accuracy and completeness of the information, the depth of the research, the coherence and organization of the essay, and the use of formal language. Consider how well they incorporated feedback from the peer review and whether their biographies effectively capture the life and achievements of the subject.

This activity helps learners develop research and writing skills, which are essential for creating detailed and engaging biographies. It enhances their ability to gather and organize information, write coherently and descriptively, and present a comprehensive account of a person's life.

Film Scene Rewrite

Objective: Learners will practice creative writing and scriptwriting by rewriting a scene from a film, enhancing their ability to understand and reinterpret dialogue, setting, and character interactions.

Level: Intermediate to Advanced

Duration: 2 hours

Materials Needed

- A selection of film scenes (printed or digital scripts)
- Film Scene Rewrite Checklist

Teaching Outline

Introduction (10 minutes)

Begin by discussing the purpose of rewriting a film scene. Explain how this activity allows learners to exercise their creativity while developing an understanding of character development, dialogue, and scene structure. Highlight the importance of maintaining coherence with the original film while introducing new elements.

Warm-Up (10 minutes)

Display examples of well-known film scenes. Watch one or two scenes and discuss their key elements, including dialogue, setting, and character interactions. Highlight how these elements contribute to the overall impact of the scene. Encourage learners to think about how they might change or enhance these elements in their own rewrite.

Choosing a Scene (10 minutes)

Ask learners to choose a scene from the provided selection. Ensure that each scene is rich in dialogue and character interactions, offering ample material for a creative rewrite. Encourage them to select a scene that interests them and sparks their imagination.

Planning the Rewrite (15 minutes)

Distribute the Film Scene Rewrite Checklist. Instruct learners to outline their rewrite, including the following aspects:

- **Setting**: Where will the scene take place? Will they keep the original setting or change it?
- **Characters**: Which characters will be in the scene? Will they introduce new characters or modify existing ones?
- **Dialogue**: How will the dialogue change? Will they add new lines, change existing ones, or introduce new interactions?
- **Plot and Actions**: What will happen in the scene? Will they change the events, introduce new conflicts, or alter the resolution?

Writing the Draft (25 minutes)

Learners write the first draft of their rewritten scene based on their outline. Encourage them to focus on creating engaging and dynamic dialogue, vivid descriptions of the setting, and coherent character interactions. Remind them to maintain the original tone and style of the film while introducing their unique changes.

Peer Review (20 minutes)

Have learners exchange their rewritten scenes with a partner. Partners review each other's work using the Film Scene Rewrite Checklist. Encourage learners to provide constructive feedback on the effectiveness of the dialogue, the creativity of the setting and plot changes, and the coherence and engagement of the scene.

Final Draft (20 minutes)

Learners revise their scenes based on the feedback received. They then write the final draft of their rewritten scene, ensuring that it is well-organized, clearly written, and properly formatted. Optionally, they can perform their scenes in front of the class, practicing their presentation and acting skills.

Reflection (10 minutes)

Conduct a class discussion on what they learned about rewriting film scenes. Facilitate a reflective discussion where learners can articulate their insights and discoveries about dialogue writing, character development, and scene structure.

Film Scene Rewrite Checklist

Setting

- Is the setting clear and well-described?
- Does the setting contribute to the overall mood of the scene?

Characters

- Are the characters' voices and personalities consistent?
- Are any new characters introduced in an interesting way?

Dialogue

- Is the dialogue engaging and natural?
- Does the dialogue effectively convey the characters' emotions?

Plot and Actions

- Are the events of the scene clear and logically structured?
- Do the changes made to the plot and actions enhance the scene?

Coherence and Engagement

- Does the rewritten scene maintain the style of the film?
- Is the scene engaging and dynamic?

Clarity and Organization

- Is the scene free of spelling and grammatical errors?
- Is the language clear and engaging?
- Is the scene well-organized and logically structured?

Assessment

Evaluate the learners' rewritten scenes based on the creativity and effectiveness of the setting and plot changes, the coherence and engagement of the dialogue, the consistency of the characters' voices and actions, the clarity and descriptiveness of the setting, and the overall organization and flow of the scene. Consider how well they incorporated feedback from the peer review and whether their scenes effectively reinterpret and enhance the original film scene.

This activity helps learners develop creative writing and scriptwriting skills, which are essential for crafting engaging and dynamic scenes. It enhances their ability to write natural and compelling dialogue, develop and adapt characters, and structure scenes coherently and engagingly.

ESL Writing Activities for Kids and Adults

FAQ Creation

Objective: Learners will practice writing clear and concise answers to frequently asked questions, enhancing their ability to communicate information effectively and anticipate the needs of an audience.

Level: Intermediate to Advanced

Duration: 2 hours

Materials Needed

- Examples of FAQ sections from various websites
- FAQ Writing Checklist

Teaching Outline

Introduction (10 minutes)

Begin by discussing the purpose and importance of FAQ sections. Explain how FAQs help to provide quick and accessible answers to common questions, improving user experience and reducing the need for direct customer support. Highlight the importance of clarity, conciseness, and anticipating user needs when writing FAQs.

Warm-Up (10 minutes)

Display examples of FAQ sections from different websites. Read a few questions and answers aloud and discuss their effectiveness. Highlight how the best FAQs are clear, concise, and directly address the users' concerns. Encourage learners to think about the types of questions that are typically included in FAQ sections and how they are answered.

ESL Writing Activities for Kids and Adults

Choosing a Topic (10 minutes)

Ask learners to choose a topic for their FAQ section. This could be a product, service, event, or any other area where people commonly have questions. Ensure that learners choose a topic they are familiar with and can generate multiple questions for.

Brainstorming Questions (10 minutes)

Instruct learners to brainstorm a list of common questions that users might have about their chosen topic. Encourage them to consider different aspects, such as features, usage, troubleshooting, and policies. Aim for a list of at least 10-15 questions.

Planning the Answers (15 minutes)

Distribute the FAQ Writing Checklist. Instruct learners to outline their answers to each question, focusing on the following aspects:

- **Clarity**: Is the answer easy to understand?
- **Conciseness**: Is the answer brief but comprehensive?
- **Relevance**: Does the answer address the question directly?
- **Tone**: Is the answer written in a user-friendly tone?

Writing the Draft (25 minutes)

Learners write the first draft of their FAQ section based on their outline. Encourage them to focus on creating clear, concise, and comprehensive answers. Remind them to anticipate any follow-up questions users might have and to provide relevant examples or additional information if necessary.

Peer Review (15 minutes)

Have learners exchange their FAQ sections with a partner. Partners review each other's work using the FAQ Writing Checklist. Encourage learners to provide constructive feedback on the clarity, conciseness, and relevance of the answers, as well as the overall organization and user-friendliness of the FAQ section.

Final Draft (15 minutes)

Learners revise their FAQs based on the feedback received. They then write the final draft of their FAQ section, ensuring that it is well-organized, clearly written, and properly formatted. Optionally, they can share their FAQs with the class, practicing their presentation and editing skills.

Reflection (10 minutes)

Conduct a class discussion on what they learned about creating FAQ sections. Facilitate a reflective discussion where learners can articulate their insights and discoveries about anticipating user needs, writing clearly and concisely, and organizing information effectively.

FAQ Writing Checklist

Clarity

- Is the answer easy to understand?
- Does the answer avoid jargon and technical language?

Conciseness

- Is the answer brief but comprehensive?
- Does the answer avoid unnecessary details?

Relevance

- Does the answer address the question directly and fully?
- Are any additional details or examples relevant and helpful?

Tone

- Is the answer written in an appropriate and user-friendly tone?
- Does the tone match the context of the FAQ section?

Organization and Structure

- Are the questions and answers well-organized?
- Are transitions between questions and answers coherent?

Clarity and Organization

- Is the FAQ section free of spelling and grammatical errors?
- Is the language clear and engaging?
- Is the FAQ section well-organized and logically structured?

Assessment

Evaluate the learners' FAQ sections based on the clarity and relevance of the answers, the conciseness and comprehensiveness of the information provided, the appropriateness and user-friendliness of the tone, and the overall organization and coherence of the FAQ section. Consider how well they incorporated feedback from the peer review and whether their FAQs effectively anticipate and address common user questions.

This activity helps learners develop effective FAQ sections. It enhances their skills in anticipating user needs, organizing information logically, and communicating complex information in an accessible way. The activity encourages critical thinking and empathy through the process of considering the user's perspective.

Press Release

Objective: Learners will practice writing a press release, improving their ability to communicate important information clearly and concisely to the media and public.

Level: Intermediate to Advanced

Duration: 2 hours

Materials Needed

- Examples of press releases (printed or digital)
- Press Release Writing Checklist

Teaching Outline

Introduction (10 minutes)

Begin by discussing the purpose and structure of a press release. Explain how press releases are used to inform the media and public about important events, announcements, or updates from an organization. Highlight the key elements of a press release: headline, dateline, introduction, body, and contact information.

Warm-Up (10 minutes)

Display examples of well-written press releases. Read a few excerpts and discuss their key elements. Highlight how effective press releases are clear, concise, and informative, providing all necessary details in a structured format. Encourage learners to think about what makes a press release engaging and newsworthy.

ESL Writing Activities for Kids and Adults

Choosing a Topic (10 minutes)

Ask learners to choose a topic for their press release. This could be an event, product launch, new hire, partnership, or any other significant announcement. Ensure that learners choose a topic they can provide detailed and accurate information about.

Planning the Press Release (15 minutes)

Distribute the Press Release Writing Checklist. Instruct learners to outline their press release, including the following sections:

- **Headline**: A clear and catchy title that summarizes the announcement.
- **Dateline**: The date and location of the release.
- **Introduction**: A brief opening paragraph that provides the most important information.
- **Body**: Detailed information about the announcement, including quotes, statistics, and other relevant details.
- **Contact Information**: Information about who to contact for more details.

Writing the Draft (25 minutes)

Learners write the first draft of their press release based on their outline. Encourage them to focus on creating a clear and engaging headline, providing essential details in the introduction, and expanding on those details in the body. Remind them to use quotes and statistics to add credibility and interest to their announcement.

Peer Review (20 minutes)

Have learners exchange their press releases with a partner. Partners review each other's work using the Press Release Writing Checklist. Encourage learners to provide constructive feedback on the clarity, conciseness, and engagement of the press release, as well as the completeness and accuracy of the information provided.

Final Draft (20 minutes)

Learners revise their press releases based on the feedback received. They then write the final draft of their press release, ensuring that it is well-organized, clearly written, and properly formatted. Optionally, they can share their press releases with the class, practicing their presentation and editing skills.

Reflection (10 minutes)

Conduct a class discussion on what they learned about writing press releases. Facilitate a reflective discussion where learners can articulate their insights and discoveries about structuring information, writing clearly and concisely, and creating engaging and newsworthy announcements.

Press Release Writing Checklist

Headline

- Is the headline clear and catchy?
- Does the headline summarize the announcement effectively?

Dateline

- Is the date and location of the release included?
- Is the dateline formatted correctly?

Introduction

- Does the introduction provide the most important information?
- Is the introduction brief and engaging?

Body

- Does the body provide detailed information about the announcement?
- Are quotes, statistics, and other relevant details included?

Contact Information

- Is the contact information complete and accurate?
- Is it clear who to contact for more details?

Clarity and Engagement

- Is the press release written in a clear and engaging manner?
- Does it effectively communicate the importance of the announcement?

Organization and Structure

- Is the press release well-organized and logically structured?
- Are transitions between sections smooth and coherent?

Clarity and Organization

- Is the press release free of spelling and grammatical errors?
- Is the language clear and engaging?
- Is the press release well-organized and logically structured?

Assessment

Evaluate the learners' press releases based on the clarity and engagement of the headline and introduction, the completeness and accuracy of the body, the relevance and impact of the quotes and statistics, the appropriateness and clarity of the contact information, and the overall organization and coherence of the press release. Consider how well they incorporated feedback from the peer review and whether their press releases effectively communicate the announcement.

This activity helps learners develop skills in writing clear, concise, and engaging press releases, which are essential for effective communication with the media and public. It enhances their ability to structure information logically, use quotes and statistics to add credibility, and anticipate the needs of their audience.

Comparative Essay

Objective: Learners will practice writing a comparative essay, enhancing their ability to analyze similarities and differences between two subjects and present their analysis clearly and effectively in written English.

Level: Intermediate to Advanced

Duration: 2 hours

Materials Needed

- Examples of comparative essays (printed or digital)
- Comparative Essay Writing Checklist

Teaching Outline

Introduction (10 minutes)

Begin by discussing the purpose and structure of a comparative essay. Explain how comparative essays analyze the similarities and differences between two subjects, providing a deeper understanding of both. Highlight the importance of a clear thesis statement, logical organization, and strong evidence to support comparisons.

Warm-Up (10 minutes)

Display examples of well-written comparative essays. Discuss their key elements, such as the introduction with a thesis statement, body paragraphs organized by either point-by-point or block method, and a conclusion that summarizes the analysis. Highlight how effective essays use clear and concise language and provide balanced comparisons.

Choosing Subjects (10 minutes)

Ask learners to choose two subjects they are interested in comparing. These could be books, movies, historical events, cultural practices, technological advancements, etc. Ensure that learners choose subjects with enough similarities and differences to analyze in detail.

Planning the Essay (15 minutes)

Distribute the Comparative Essay Writing Checklist. Instruct learners to outline their essay, including the following sections:

- **Introduction**: Introduce the two subjects and present a clear thesis statement.
- **Body Paragraphs**: Organize the body paragraphs using either the point-by-point method (alternating points about each subject) or the block method (discussing all points about one subject, then all points about the other).
- **Conclusion**: Summarize the main points of comparison and restate the thesis in a new light.

Writing the Draft (25 minutes)

Learners write the first draft of their comparative essay based on their outline. Encourage them to focus on providing clear and balanced comparisons, using evidence and examples to support their analysis. Remind them to maintain coherence and logical flow throughout the essay.

Peer Review (20 minutes)

Have learners exchange their essays with a partner. Partners review each other's work using the Comparative Essay Writing Checklist.

Encourage learners to provide constructive feedback on the clarity, coherence, and effectiveness of the essay, as well as the strength of the comparisons and the organization of the content.

Final Draft (20 minutes)

Learners revise their essays based on the feedback received. They then write the final draft of their comparative essay, ensuring that it is well-organized, clearly written, and effectively analyzes the similarities and differences between the two subjects. Optionally, they can share their essays with the class, practicing their presentation and communication skills.

Reflection (10 minutes)

Conduct a class discussion on what they learned about writing comparative essays. Facilitate a reflective discussion where learners can articulate their insights and discoveries about analyzing subjects, using evidence to support comparisons, and organizing essays effectively.

Comparative Essay Writing Checklist

Introduction

- Does the introduction provide a clear overview of the two subjects being compared?
- Is there a strong thesis statement that outlines the main points of comparison?

Body Paragraphs

- Are the body paragraphs organized using either the point-by-point or block method?
- Are the comparisons clear and well-supported with evidence and examples?
- Is there a balance between the discussion of both subjects?

Conclusion

- Does the conclusion summarize the main points of comparison?
- Is the thesis restated in a new light?
- Are the final thoughts insightful and conclusive?

Clarity and Accuracy

- Is the essay written in a clear and concise manner?
- Is the information accurate and free of errors?

Organization and Flow

- Is the essay well-organized and logically structured?
- Are transitions between sections smooth and coherent?

Assessment

Evaluate the learners' comparative essays based on the clarity and accuracy of the introduction, the effectiveness and balance of the body paragraphs, the relevance and clarity of the conclusion, and the overall organization and coherence of the essay. Consider how well they incorporated feedback from the peer review and whether their essays effectively analyze the similarities and differences between the two subjects.

This activity helps learners develop skills in critical thinking and analytical writing by comparing and contrasting two subjects. It enhances their ability to organize information logically, use evidence to support their analysis, and present their ideas clearly.

ESL WRITING ACTIVITIES FOR KIDS AND ADULTS

Infographic Analysis

Objective: Learners will practice analyzing infographics, enhancing their ability to interpret data, draw insights, and present their analysis clearly and effectively in written English.

Level: Intermediate to Advanced

Duration: 2 hours

Materials Needed

- Examples of infographics (printed or digital)
- Infographic Analysis Writing Checklist

Teaching Outline

Introduction (10 minutes)

Begin by discussing the purpose and importance of infographics. Explain how infographics combine visual elements and text to present data in a clear and engaging manner. Highlight the role of analysis in understanding the effectiveness and impact of an infographic.

Warm-Up (10 minutes)

Display examples of well-designed infographics. Discuss their key elements, such as layout, color scheme, data visualization techniques, and the clarity of the message. Highlight how effective infographics use visuals to simplify complex information and engage the audience. Encourage learners to think about what makes an infographic both visually appealing and informative.

Choosing an Infographic (10 minutes)

Ask learners to choose an infographic from the examples provided or find one online that interests them. Ensure that learners choose infographics with clear data and visuals they can analyze in detail.

Analyzing the Infographic (15 minutes)

Distribute the Infographic Analysis Writing Checklist. Instruct learners to analyze their chosen infographic, considering the following questions:

- What is the main topic or theme of the infographic?
- What key data or information is presented?
- How are the visuals used to convey the information?
- Is the infographic effective in communicating its message? Why or why not?
- What conclusions or insights can be drawn from the data?

Writing the Draft (25 minutes)

Learners write the first draft of their infographic analysis based on their analysis. Encourage them to focus on providing a clear and concise overview of the infographic, explaining the key data and visuals, and evaluating the effectiveness of the infographic. Remind them to use descriptive and analytical language and organize their writing logically.

Peer Review (20 minutes)

Have learners exchange their infographic analyses with a partner. Partners review each other's work using the Infographic Analysis Writing Checklist. Encourage learners to provide constructive feedback on the clarity, accuracy, and effectiveness of the analysis, as well as the organization and flow of the writing.

Final Draft (20 minutes)

Learners revise their infographic analyses based on the feedback received. They then write the final draft of their analysis, ensuring that it is well-organized, clearly written, and effectively evaluates the infographic. Optionally, they can share their analyses with the class, practicing their presentation and communication skills.

Reflection (10 minutes)

Conduct a class discussion on what they learned about analyzing infographics. Facilitate a reflective discussion where learners can articulate their insights and discoveries about interpreting data, evaluating visuals, and presenting analyses effectively.

Infographic Analysis Writing Checklist

Introduction

- Does the introduction provide a clear overview of the topic?
- Is the purpose of the infographic stated?

Key Data and Visuals

- Are the key data points and visuals accurately described?
- Is the relationship between the visuals and the data explained?

Effectiveness Evaluation

- Is the effectiveness of the infographic in communicating its message evaluated?
- Are strengths and weaknesses of the infographic discussed?

Conclusions and Insights

- Are important conclusions or insights drawn from the data?
- Are these conclusions clearly supported by the data?

Clarity and Accuracy

- Is the analysis written in a clear and concise manner?
- Is the information accurate and free of errors?

Organization and Flow

- Is the analysis well-organized and logically structured?
- Are transitions between sections smooth and coherent?

Assessment

Evaluate the learners' infographic analyses based on the clarity and accuracy of the introduction, the effectiveness of the key data and visuals section, the relevance and clarity of the effectiveness evaluation and conclusions, and the overall organization and coherence of the analysis. Consider how well they incorporated feedback from the peer review and whether their analyses effectively evaluate the infographic.

This activity helps learners develop skills in interpreting and analyzing visual data, which is essential for effective communication in various fields. It enhances their ability to critically evaluate the effectiveness of visual presentations, use descriptive and analytical language, and present their analyses clearly.

ESL Writing Activities for Kids and Adults

ESL Writing Activities for Kids and Adults

Local Event Report

Objective: Learners will practice writing a report on a local event, improving their ability to observe, record, and communicate detailed and accurate information.

Level: Intermediate to Advanced

Duration: 2 hours

Materials Needed

- Examples of local event reports (printed or digital)
- Local Event Report Checklist

Teaching Outline

Introduction (10 minutes)

Begin by discussing the purpose and structure of a local event report. Explain how such reports provide a detailed account of events, informing the community about what happened, who was involved, and the significance of the event. Highlight the key elements of a report: headline, introduction, body, and conclusion.

Warm-Up (10 minutes)

Display examples of well-written local event reports. Read a few excerpts and discuss their key elements. Highlight how effective reports are clear, concise, and informative, providing all necessary details in a structured format. Encourage learners to think about what makes a report engaging and newsworthy.

Choosing an Event (10 minutes)

Ask learners to choose a local event to report on. This could be a community gathering, concert, festival, sports event, or any other significant local occurrence. Ensure that learners choose an event they are familiar with or can research thoroughly.

Planning the Report (15 minutes)

Distribute the Local Event Report Checklist. Instruct learners to outline their report, including the following sections:

- **Headline**: A clear and catchy title that summarizes the event.
- **Introduction**: A brief opening paragraph that provides the most important information about the event.
- **Body**: Detailed information about the event, including descriptions of activities, quotes from participants, and any relevant statistics.
- **Conclusion**: A summary of the event's significance and any future implications.

Writing the Draft (25 minutes)

Learners write the first draft of their event report based on their outline. Encourage them to focus on creating a clear and engaging headline, providing essential details in the introduction, and expanding on those details in the body. Remind them to include quotes and observations to add depth to their report.

Peer Review (20 minutes)

Have learners exchange their reports with a partner. Partners review each other's work using the Local Event Report Checklist. Encourage learners to provide constructive feedback on the clarity, conciseness, and engagement of the report, as well as the completeness and accuracy of the information provided.

Final Draft (20 minutes)

Learners revise their reports based on the feedback received. They then write the final draft of their event report, ensuring that it is well-organized, clearly written, and properly formatted. Optionally, they can share their reports with the class, practicing their presentation and editing skills.

Reflection (10 minutes)

Conduct a class discussion on what they learned about writing local event reports. Facilitate a reflective discussion where learners can articulate their insights and discoveries about structuring information, writing clearly and concisely, and creating engaging and informative reports.

Local Event Report Checklist

Headline

- Is the headline clear and catchy?
- Does the headline summarize the event effectively?

Introduction

- Does the introduction provide the most important information?
- Is the introduction brief and engaging?

Body

- Does the body provide detailed information about the event?
- Are quotes, observations, and relevant statistics included?

Conclusion

- Does the conclusion summarize the event's significance?
- Are any future implications or follow-up events mentioned?

Clarity and Engagement

- Is the report written in a clear and engaging manner?
- Does it effectively communicate the importance of the event?

Organization and Structure

- Is the report well-organized and logically structured?
- Are transitions between sections smooth and coherent?

Clarity and Organization

- Is the report free of spelling and grammatical errors?
- Is the language clear and engaging?
- Is the report well-organized and logically structured?

Assessment

Evaluate the learners' reports based on the clarity and engagement of the headline and introduction, the completeness and accuracy of the body, the relevance and impact of the quotes and observations, the effectiveness of the conclusion, and the overall organization and coherence of the report. Consider how well they incorporated feedback from the peer review and whether their reports effectively communicate the event.

This activity helps learners develop skills in writing clear, concise, and engaging event reports, which are essential for effective communication with the public. It enhances their ability to structure information logically, use quotes and observations to add depth, and anticipate the needs of their audience.

Comic Strip Dialogue

Objective: Learners will practice writing dialogue for a comic strip, enhancing their ability to create engaging, concise, and expressive conversations in written form.

Level: Intermediate to Advanced

Duration: 2 hours

Materials Needed

- Examples of comic strips (printed or digital)
- Blank comic strip templates
- Comic Strip Dialogue Writing Checklist

Teaching Outline

Introduction (10 minutes)

Begin by discussing the purpose and structure of a comic strip. Explain how comic strips use a combination of images and dialogue to tell a story or convey a message. Highlight the importance of writing dialogue that is concise, expressive, and suited to the characters and situations depicted.

Warm-Up (10 minutes)

Display examples of well-written comic strips. Read a few excerpts and discuss their key elements. Highlight how effective comic strips use dialogue to advance the plot, reveal character, and create humor or drama. Encourage learners to think about what makes dialogue engaging and how it interacts with the visual elements of a comic strip.

Choosing a Scenario (10 minutes)

Ask learners to choose or create a scenario for their comic strip. This could be a simple everyday situation, a humorous event, or a dramatic moment. Ensure that learners choose a scenario that allows for interesting and varied dialogue.

Planning the Dialogue (15 minutes)

Distribute the Comic Strip Dialogue Writing Checklist. Instruct learners to outline their comic strip, including the following aspects:

- **Characters**: Who are the characters involved in the dialogue?
- **Setting**: Where does the scene take place?
- **Plot**: What is happening in the scene?
- **Dialogue**: What do the characters say to each other? How does the dialogue advance the plot or reveal character?

Writing the Draft (25 minutes)

Learners write the first draft of their comic strip dialogue based on their outline. Encourage them to focus on creating dialogue that is concise, expressive, and appropriate for the characters and situation. Remind them to consider how the dialogue interacts with the visual elements of the comic strip.

Peer Review (20 minutes)

Have learners exchange their comic strips with a partner. Partners review each other's work using the Comic Strip Dialogue Writing Checklist. Encourage learners to provide constructive feedback on the clarity, expressiveness, and engagement of the dialogue, as well as the effectiveness of the interaction between dialogue and visuals.

Final Draft (20 minutes)

Learners revise their comic strips based on the feedback received. They then write the final draft of their dialogue, ensuring that it is well-organized, clearly written, and properly formatted within the comic strip template. Optionally, they can share their comic strips with the class, practicing their presentation and editing skills.

Reflection (10 minutes)

Conduct a class discussion on what they learned about writing comic strip dialogue. Facilitate a reflective discussion where learners can articulate their insights and discoveries about creating engaging and expressive dialogue, using concise language, and integrating dialogue with visual elements.

ESL WRITING ACTIVITIES FOR KIDS AND ADULTS

Comic Strip Dialogue Writing Checklist

Characters

- Are the characters clearly defined?
- Is the dialogue appropriate for each character?

Setting

- Is the setting clear and relevant to the scene?
- Does the setting enhance the dialogue and plot?

Plot

- Does the dialogue advance the plot or reveal character?
- Is the plot clear and engaging?

Dialogue

- Is the dialogue concise and expressive?
- Does the dialogue interact effectively with the visual elements?

Clarity and Engagement

- Is the dialogue easy to follow and understand?
- Is the dialogue engaging and interesting?

Organization and Structure

- Is the comic strip well-organized and logically structured?
- Are transitions between panels smooth and coherent?

Clarity and Organization

- Is the comic strip free of spelling and grammatical errors?
- Is the language clear and engaging?
- Is the comic strip well-organized and logically structured?

Assessment

Evaluate the learners' comic strips based on the clarity and expressiveness of the dialogue, the effectiveness of the interaction between dialogue and visual elements, the engagement and interest of the plot, and the overall organization and coherence of the comic strip. Consider how well they incorporated feedback from the peer review and whether their comic strips effectively communicate the scenario.

This activity helps learners develop skills in writing concise, expressive, and engaging dialogue, which is essential for creating effective comic strips. It enhances their ability to integrate written and visual elements, use language creatively, and develop character and plot through dialogue.

Petition Writing

Objective: Learners will practice writing a petition to advocate for a cause, enhancing their ability to persuade and communicate effectively in written English.

Level: Intermediate to Advanced

Duration: 2 hours

Materials Needed

- Examples of petitions (printed or digital)
- Petition Writing Checklist

Teaching Outline

Introduction (10 minutes)

Begin by discussing the purpose and structure of a petition. Explain how petitions are used to advocate for changes by gathering support from the public. Highlight the key elements of a petition: title, introduction, body, call to action, and signatures.

Warm-Up (10 minutes)

Display examples of well-written petitions. Read a few excerpts and discuss their key elements. Highlight how effective petitions clearly state the issue, provide compelling reasons for support, and include a clear call to action. Encourage learners to think about what makes a petition persuasive and effective.

ESL Writing Activities for Kids and Adults

Choosing a Cause (10 minutes)

Ask learners to choose a cause they are passionate about. This could be a local community issue, an environmental concern, a social justice matter, or any other cause they feel strongly about. Ensure that learners choose a topic they can provide detailed and persuasive arguments for.

Planning the Petition (15 minutes)

Distribute the Petition Writing Checklist. Instruct learners to outline their petition, including the following sections:

- **Title**: A clear and concise title that summarizes the cause.
- **Introduction**: A brief opening paragraph that introduces the issue and its importance.
- **Body**: Detailed arguments supporting the cause, including facts, statistics, and personal stories.
- **Call to Action**: A clear statement of what the petition is asking for and how people can help.
- **Signatures**: Space for supporters to sign and show their support.

Writing the Draft (25 minutes)

Learners write the first draft of their petition based on their outline. Encourage them to focus on creating a compelling introduction, providing strong and persuasive arguments in the body, and ending with a clear and motivating call to action. Remind them to use facts, statistics, and personal stories to add credibility and emotional appeal.

Peer Review (20 minutes)

Have learners exchange their petitions with a partner. Partners review each other's work using the Petition Writing Checklist. Encourage learners to provide constructive feedback on the clarity, persuasiveness, and engagement of the petition, as well as the completeness and accuracy of the information provided.

Final Draft (20 minutes)

Learners revise their petitions based on the feedback received. They then write the final draft of their petition, ensuring that it is well-organized, clearly written, and properly formatted. Optionally, they can share their petitions with the class, practicing their presentation and editing skills.

Reflection (10 minutes)

Conduct a class discussion on what they learned about writing petitions. Facilitate a reflective discussion where learners can articulate their insights and discoveries about structuring arguments, writing persuasively, and creating clear calls to action.

Petition Writing Checklist

Title

- Is the title clear and concise?
- Does the title effectively summarize the cause?

Introduction

- Does the introduction clearly state the issue?
- Is the introduction engaging and informative?

Body

- Does the body provide detailed and persuasive arguments?
- Are facts, statistics, and personal stories included?

Call to Action

- Is the call to action clear and motivating?
- Does it clearly state what the petition is asking for and how people can help?

Signatures

- Is there space provided for supporters to sign?
- Is it clear how people can show their support?

Clarity and Persuasiveness

- Is the petition written in a clear and persuasive manner?
- Does it effectively communicate the importance of the cause?

Organization and Structure

- Is the petition well-organized and logically structured?
- Are transitions between sections smooth and coherent?

Clarity and Organization

- Is the petition free of spelling and grammatical errors?
- Is the language clear and engaging?
- Is the petition well-organized and logically structured?

Assessment

Evaluate the learners' petitions based on the clarity and engagement of the title and introduction, the persuasiveness and completeness of the body, the effectiveness of the call to action, and the overall organization and coherence of the petition. Consider how well they incorporated feedback from the peer review and whether their petitions effectively communicate the cause and motivate action.

This activity helps learners develop skills in writing clear, persuasive, and engaging petitions, which are essential for effective advocacy and communication. It enhances their ability to structure arguments logically, use facts and stories to add credibility, and create motivating calls to action.

Cover Letter

Objective: Learners will practice writing a cover letter for a job application, enhancing their ability to introduce themselves, highlight their qualifications, and communicate professionally in written English.

Level: Intermediate to Advanced

Duration: 2 hours

Materials Needed

- Examples of cover letters (printed or digital)
- Cover Letter Writing Checklist

Teaching Outline

Introduction (10 minutes)

Begin by discussing the purpose and structure of a cover letter. Explain how cover letters introduce applicants to potential employers, highlight relevant skills and experiences, and express interest in the position. Highlight the importance of tailoring cover letters to specific job descriptions and company cultures.

Warm-Up (10 minutes)

Display examples of well-written cover letters. Read a few excerpts and discuss their key elements. Highlight how effective cover letters address the employer's needs, showcase relevant qualifications, and convey enthusiasm for the position. Encourage learners to think about what makes a cover letter compelling and persuasive.

ESL Writing Activities for Kids and Adults

Choosing a Job Position (10 minutes)

Ask learners to choose a job position they are interested in applying for or imagine a position they would like to apply to. Ensure that learners choose a position they can provide relevant qualifications and experiences for.

Planning the Cover Letter (15 minutes)

Distribute the Cover Letter Writing Checklist. Instruct learners to outline their cover letter, including the following sections:

- **Header**: Contact information and date
- **Salutation**: Greeting to the hiring manager
- **Introduction**: Introduction of self and purpose of the letter
- **Body**: Highlighting relevant qualifications and experiences
- **Closing**: Expression of gratitude and call to action

Writing the Draft (25 minutes)

Learners write the first draft of their cover letter based on their outline. Encourage them to focus on addressing the employer's needs, showcasing their qualifications and experiences, and expressing enthusiasm for the position. Remind them to use professional language and tailor their letter to the specific job description.

Peer Review (20 minutes)

Have learners exchange their cover letters with a partner. Partners review each other's work using the Cover Letter Writing Checklist. Encourage learners to provide constructive feedback on the clarity, relevance, and professionalism of the cover letter, as well as the effectiveness of the language and tone.

Final Draft (20 minutes)

Learners revise their cover letters based on the feedback received. They then write the final draft of their cover letter, ensuring that it is well-organized, clearly written, and properly formatted. Optionally, they can share their cover letters with the class, practicing their presentation and communication skills.

Reflection (10 minutes)

Conduct a class discussion on what they learned about writing cover letters. Facilitate a reflective discussion where learners can articulate their insights and discoveries about showcasing qualifications, tailoring letters to specific positions, and expressing enthusiasm professionally.

ESL Writing Activities for Kids and Adults

Cover Letter Writing Checklist

Header

- Is the contact information and date included?
- Is the header formatted correctly?

Salutation

- Is the greeting appropriate and addressed to the hiring manager?
- Is the salutation formatted correctly?

Introduction

- Does the introduction introduce the applicant and the purpose of the letter?
- Is the introduction engaging and professional?

Body

- Does the body highlight relevant qualifications and experiences?
- Are achievements and skills showcased effectively?
- Is the body tailored to the specific job description?

Closing

- Does the closing express gratitude and enthusiasm?
- Is there a clear call to action for next steps?
- Is the closing formatted correctly?

Clarity and Professionalism

- Is the cover letter written in a clear and professional manner?
- Is the language appropriate for a job application?
- Does the cover letter showcase the applicant's professionalism?

Organization and Structure

- Is the cover letter well-organized and logically structured?
- Are transitions between sections smooth and coherent?

Clarity and Organization

- Is the cover letter free of spelling and grammatical errors?
- Is the language clear and engaging?
- Is the cover letter well-organized and logically structured?

Assessment

Evaluate the learners' cover letters based on the clarity and professionalism of the header and salutation, the relevance and effectiveness of the body, the enthusiasm and professionalism of the closing, and the overall organization and coherence of the cover letter. Consider how well they incorporated feedback from the peer review and whether their cover letters effectively communicate their qualifications and interest in the position.

This activity helps learners develop skills in writing professional and persuasive cover letters, which are essential for job applications and career advancement. It enhances their ability to showcase relevant qualifications and experiences, tailor letters to specific job descriptions, and express enthusiasm for potential job positions.

ESL WRITING ACTIVITIES FOR KIDS AND ADULTS

Resume Writing

Objective: Learners will practice writing a resume, highlighting their skills, experiences, and qualifications for a specific job or career path, enhancing their ability to present themselves effectively in written English.

Level: Intermediate to Advanced

Duration: 2 hours

Materials Needed

- Examples of resumes (printed or digital)
- Resume Writing Checklist

Teaching Outline

Introduction (10 minutes)

Begin by discussing the purpose and importance of a resume. Explain how resumes serve as a marketing tool for job seekers, showcasing their skills, experiences, and qualifications to potential employers. Highlight the key components of a resume and the importance of tailoring it to specific job descriptions.

Warm-Up (10 minutes)

Display examples of well-written resumes. Discuss their key elements, such as layout, formatting, and content organization. Highlight how effective resumes use clear and concise language, prioritize relevant information, and present qualifications in a compelling manner.

ESL Writing Activities for Kids and Adults

Encourage learners to think about what makes a resume stand out to employers.

Choosing a Job Position (10 minutes)

Ask learners to choose a job position they are interested in applying for or imagine a position they would like to apply to. Ensure that learners choose a position they can provide relevant skills and experiences for.

Planning the Resume (15 minutes)

Distribute the Resume Writing Checklist. Instruct learners to outline their resume, including the following sections:

- **Header**: Contact information and professional summary
- **Skills**: Key skills and competencies relevant to the job
- **Experience**: Work history, internships, volunteer experiences, etc.
- **Education**: Academic background, degrees, certifications, etc.
- **Additional Sections**: Optional sections such as achievements, awards, languages, etc.

Writing the Draft (25 minutes)

Learners write the first draft of their resume based on their outline. Encourage them to focus on highlighting their most relevant skills and experiences, using action verbs to describe their accomplishments, and organizing information in a clear and structured manner. Remind them to tailor their resume to the specific job description and company culture.

Peer Review (20 minutes)

Have learners exchange their resumes with a partner. Partners review each other's work using the Resume Writing Checklist. Encourage learners to provide constructive feedback on the clarity, relevance, and professionalism of the resume, as well as the effectiveness of the language and formatting.

Final Draft (20 minutes)

Learners revise their resumes based on the feedback received. They then write the final draft of their resume, ensuring that it is well-organized, clearly written, and properly formatted. Optionally, they can share their resumes with the class, practicing their presentation and communication skills.

Reflection (10 minutes)

Conduct a class discussion on what they learned about writing resumes. Facilitate a reflective discussion where learners can articulate their insights and discoveries about presenting qualifications, tailoring resumes to specific positions, and formatting documents professionally.

Resume Writing Checklist

Header

- Is the contact information included and formatted correctly?
- Does the professional summary effectively introduce the applicant?

Skills

- Are the key skills relevant to the job highlighted?
- Are skills presented in a clear and organized manner?

Experience

- Does the work history effectively showcase relevant experiences and accomplishments?
- Are action verbs used to describe achievements and responsibilities?

Education

- Is the academic background clearly presented?
- Are degrees, certifications, and relevant coursework included?

Additional Sections

- Are optional sections such as achievements, awards, languages, etc., included if relevant?
- Do additional sections add value to the resume without overcrowding it?

Clarity and Professionalism

- Is the resume written in a clear and professional manner?
- Is the language appropriate for a job application?
- Does the resume showcase the applicant's professionalism?

Organization and Structure

- Is the resume well-organized and logically structured?
- Are sections and subsections clearly delineated?

Clarity and Organization

- Is the resume free of spelling and grammatical errors?
- Is the language clear and engaging?
- Is the resume well-organized and logically structured?

Assessment

Evaluate the learners' resumes based on the clarity and professionalism of the header and professional summary, the relevance and effectiveness of the skills and experience sections, the clarity and organization of the education and additional sections, and the overall organization and coherence of the resume. Consider how well they incorporated feedback from the peer review and whether their resumes effectively showcase their qualifications and suitability for the position.

This activity helps learners develop skills in writing professional and persuasive resumes, which are essential for job applications and career advancement. It enhances their ability to showcase relevant skills and experiences, tailor resumes to specific job descriptions, and present qualifications in a compelling manner.

Book Review

What did you think of *ESL Writing Activities for Kids and Adults*?

Please leave a review of the book on Amazon!

New ESL Books

Order new books via the *ESL Expat* website – or directly from Amazon.

Visit *ESL Expat* online for updated materials, new games, activity books and more resources for teaching English language learners.

ESLexpat.com

Made in United States
Orlando, FL
27 February 2025